Fátima Aparecida R. R. Guimarães
Rosângela Lopes Borges
Rainara M. da Silva

School management

Fátima Aparecida R. R. Guimarães
Rosângela Lopes Borges
Rainara M. da Silva

School management

Profile of the headmasters of municipal schools in the city of Caldas Novas/GO

ScienciaScripts

Imprint

Any brand names and product names mentioned in this book are subject to trademark, brand or patent protection and are trademarks or registered trademarks of their respective holders. The use of brand names, product names, common names, trade names, product descriptions etc. even without a particular marking in this work is in no way to be construed to mean that such names may be regarded as unrestricted in respect of trademark and brand protection legislation and could thus be used by anyone.

Cover image: www.ingimage.com

This book is a translation from the original published under ISBN 978-613-9-72723-0.

Publisher:
Sciencia Scripts
is a trademark of
Dodo Books Indian Ocean Ltd. and OmniScriptum S.R.L publishing group

120 High Road, East Finchley, London, N2 9ED, United Kingdom
Str. Armeneasca 28/1, office 1, Chisinau MD-2012, Republic of Moldova, Europe
Printed at: see last page
ISBN: 978-620-7-89946-3

Copyright © Fátima Aparecida R. R. Guimarães, Rosângela Lopes Borges, Rainara M. da Silva
Copyright © 2024 Dodo Books Indian Ocean Ltd. and OmniScriptum S.R.L publishing group

Fátima Aparecida Rodrigues Ribeiro Guimarães

Degree in Portuguese/English Literature (Morrinhos Faculty of Education, Sciences and Letters (1998); Postgraduate in Teaching Methodologies (UFU, 2001); Postgraduate in Portuguese Language (USO, 2003); Specialisation in Educational Administration (UNIVERSO, 2010); Master's in Educational Sciences (Universidad Maria Serrana, 2017); PhD student in Educational Sciences (Universidad Del Sol).
fatimarrguimaraes@hotmail.com

Rosângela Lopes Borges

Graduated in Languages (Port./Ing.) (UEG, 2006); Postgraduate in Special Education (APOGEU, 2010); LIBRAS interpreter (ASG, 2011); Specialisation in Clinical and Institutional Psychopedagogy (UNINTER, 2017); Master's student in Professional and Technological Education (IFGoiano). She is currently a university lecturer and part of the Multidisciplinary Team of the Specialised Psychopedagogical Care Centre - NAPE, at the Caldas Novas College, in the state of Goiás, Brazil. rosalb2@hotmail.com

Rainara Martins Da Silva

Degree in Pedagogy from Faculdade de Caldas Novas (UNICALDAS, 2018); Postgraduate student in Specialised Educational Assistance (AEE) (UNICESUMAR).
ra.rainara@hotmail.com

INDICE

INTRODUCTION

Education in our country began in colonial Brazil, with the arrival of the Jesuits who sought to catechise the Indians in order to prophesy the Christian faith and "save" the aborigines from hell. After the Royal Family moved to Brazil, education began to take a new direction, but it wasn't until the creation of the Magna Carta in 1946 that education for all was realised.

In 1961, the first National Education Guidelines and Bases Law was instituted, later reformulated in 1971. Education became the right of all and the duty of the state and the family with the Federative Constitution of Brazil. And in 1996, the LDB was extended in such a way that it is still used to guide education today.

After the creation of these documents, Brazilian education came to be structured as Basic Education, which encompasses Early Childhood Education, Primary Education and Basic Education. These involve the ages of 4 months to 17 years on average. These organisations have been improving and requiring more competent administrators to take them on.

The Industrial Revolution contributed significantly to a change in the concept of leadership and management. This was because the aim was to optimise results and not just make a profit. Hence the beginning of what is known today as management.

It is known that this terminology is ancestral to the emergence of the school itself. The concept of school management was created to overcome the possible narrow focus of the term school administration. It is broader in scope, as it has its own culture and identity, and is capable of reacting effectively to the demands of the local contexts in which it operates.

Since it was created, management has gone from traditional (linked to hierarchy, bureaucratic and mechanistic) to modern management (employees are now seen as real human beings) to contemporary management (an indeterminate and organised approach). The latter sought to adapt to society and new technologies.

Educational management is based on the organisation of federal, state and municipal education systems and their obligations. While school management encompasses all of the institution's practices, the manager is therefore responsible for organising and developing the school, drawing up, executing and coordinating projects and plans.

School management is divided into three distinct but concomitant areas. These are Pedagogical School Management, which determines teaching objectives, Administrative School Management, which is concerned with institutional and physical care, and Human Resources School Management, which is concerned with the school's relationship with pupils' parents, pupils and teachers.

In addition to these, there is School Time Management, which is the organisation of the manager's time and availability, School Communication Management, which refers to care and dedication to dialogue, and lastly, Financial Management, which is the administrator's job to manage the school's financial resources.

It is understood that for institutions to function properly, there needs to be a proper process of school organisation and development. To do this, the school manager must use pedagogical planning, based on the evaluations of the previous period and their self-evaluations.

To be a good school manager, the professional must have good educational leadership, have flexibility and autonomy, support the community, create a good school climate, be involved in the teaching-learning process, know and participate in the evaluation of academic performance, be able to supervise teachers, know and be up-to-date with teaching support materials and texts, and provide a physical space suitable for teaching.

Modernity demands managers who are more dynamic, creative and capable of interpreting the demands of the moment and providing more suitable teaching-learning conditions at school. To this end, it is essential for school managers to have good training, which implies a good planning process for changes and innovations in the school.

It is understood that a comprehensive and interdisciplinary training process encourages school work, strengthening autonomy through organised, humane and democratic work. With this in mind, school managers can encourage and even create Student Councils and Guilds, using them to their advantage.

It is recognised that improving the quality of teaching is related to autonomous management, considering the content, method and coexistence between the participants in the teaching-learning process to be inseparable. The initial hypothesis was that the managers (headmasters) of the municipal schools in Caldas Novas, Goiás - Brazil, did not have adequate training for the job and that this prevented them from exercising truly democratic management.

We then set out to interview the headmasters of these schools, as well as the teachers and students, in order to ascertain their academic backgrounds and the method used to get into their positions. To see if their management is truly democratic. To analyse the perception of the teachers and students in relation to the management carried out by the current headmaster.

In view of the importance of the subject for schools and society in general, this study is organised into five chapters: Chapter I - Protocol Framework; Chapter II - Theoretical Framework; Chapter III - Methodological Framework; Chapter IV - Analytical Framework and Chapter V - Conclusion. Then there are the References, Appendices and Annexes.

It is hoped that this reading can contribute to the intellectual and personal growth of the readers, be they teachers, parents, students or headmasters. It is also hoped that this reading can bring about significant changes in school management, so that it becomes more democratic and participatory.

CHAPTER 1

PROTOCOL MILESTONE

1.1 DESCRIPTION OF THE PROBLEM

Article 206 of the Federal Constitution (1988) described the democratisation of public education policies, with the democratic management of public education as one of its basic principles.

The National Education Guidelines and Bases Law - LDB (1996) also included democratic management of public education in its articles. It establishes that education systems will define the norms for the democratic management of education in accordance with their peculiarities and with the principle of the participation of school communities.

The National Education Plan (2010) embraces the democratic management of education along with the dissemination of the principles of equity and respect for diversity. The strategy to fulfil this goal, listed as 19, which deals with the commissioned appointment of school headmasters, is the application of a specific national test in order to subsidise the definition of objective criteria for the appointment of school headmasters, putting an end to political appointment once and for all.

According to Honorato (2012), when it comes to the management of a school institution, three issues must be addressed: The first is the possibility of the election for the position of headmaster being open to the community. The second is the financial resources made available directly to the school, with the apparent autonomy of this management, and the third is the effective participation of the external community in pedagogical and administrative decision-making.

It is known that a good manager is one who values the participation of the school community in the decision-making process, in the collective construction of school objectives and practices, in dialogue and in the search for consensus (LIBÂNEO, 2008).

In view of the dimension that the subject assumes for Brazilian education and consequently for society in general, the following problem arises: What is the profile of the professionals (headmasters) who take over the management of municipal schools in the city of Caldas Novas, Goiás?

1.2 RESEARCH QUESTIONS
1.2.1 General Questions

What is the profile of headmasters who take over the management of municipal schools in the city of Caldas Novas, Goiás?

1.2.2 Secondary Questions

What academic training, training courses and tests did the director have to take in order to fulfil his role?

How important is school management training for a head teacher?

How are headmasters and their management perceived by students and teachers?

1.3 RESEARCH OBJECTIVES
1.3.1 General Objective

To analyse the profile and management of the headmasters of municipal schools in the city of Caldas Novas, Goiás.

1.3.2 Specific objectives

Observing the importance of democratic and participatory management for school management.

Investigate whether the directors' academic qualifications and training are compatible with the position they hold.

To analyse the perception of teachers and students in relation to the management carried out by the current headmaster.

1.4 BACKGROUND

This study is justified by the importance of the educational manager (headmaster) in the school environment. Deluiz (1996) says that this professional must have the ability to apply knowledge and/or skills to solve a problem in a given situation and, where relevant, demonstrable personal attributes.

It is understood that school management, in pursuit of quality education for all, is assuming and demanding more than mere centralising and technical administration. Scholars such as Luck (2009) have listed nine democratic and participatory management competences inherent to the school headmaster.

According to Paro (2003), in his research, the greatest qualities of a school manager are more closely linked to their dedication, commitment and involvement with the different areas of the school. In addition: knowing how to listen, being a mediator, having a spirit of leadership and enjoying what they do.

For management to be effectively democratic and efficient, the person who has taken on this role needs to be trained for it. It is understood that academic training, retraining and continuous participation in school management courses are of the utmost importance for school managers to be able to carry out their duties well. This justifies a study into the profile of professionals currently managing schools in Caldas Novas, Goiás.

1.5 DELIMITATION AND LIMITATION

The aim was to carry out a survey of the headmasters of municipal schools in the city of Caldas Novas, Goiás, Brazil, in order to find out the profile of the professionals who manage schools in this municipality.

The instruments used in this study were obtained specifically from the 18 municipal schools in the city of Caldas Novas.

The author of this project has free access to the 18 educational institutions because she is the technical pedagogical advisor to the Municipal Education Council. It is understood that this position facilitated access to the data that was investigated.

CHAPTER 2

THEORETICAL FRAMEWORK

2.1 CONCEPTUAL FRAMEWORK

Profile: Set of characteristics or competences required to perform an activity, position or function.

Director: A person whose job it is to run different organisations or institutions, such as a company or educational establishment. Their main task is to direct the staff under their control and guide them in the best possible way to achieve the set objective.

School management: An expression related to action that aims to promote the organisation, mobilisation and articulation of all the material and human conditions necessary to guarantee progress in the socio-educational processes of educational establishments, geared towards the effective promotion of learning.

2.2 HISTORIC MILESTONE

The term "management" is older than the creation or emergence of "school". It can be traced back to the hieroglyphs of ancient Egypt, as well as the works of classical Greco-Roman authors such as Homer, Plato, Cicero, Plutarch and Marcus Aurelius. These works presented the responsibilities of leaders and how they should behave (HONORATO, 2012).

The Industrial Revolution in the 18th century contributed to a change in the concept of leadership. It required the development of innovative behaviours between owners, foremen and employees in order to optimise production processes. Before that, the relationship between boss and employees was perversely tyrannical and aimed purely at financial profit (BASS, 2008).

The concept of school management was created to overcome a possible narrow focus on the term school administration. It arose from the country's political opening movements, which began to promote new concepts and values, associated above all with the idea of school autonomy, the participation of society and the community, the creation of community, co-operative and associative schools and the promotion of parents' associations. Thus, in the context of school management, the educational establishment came to be seen as an open system with its own culture and identity, capable of reacting effectively to the demands of the local contexts in which it operates.

According to Luck (2000, p.02) there are nine indicators of good school management: educational leadership, flexibility and autonomy, community support, school climate, the teaching-learning process, assessment of academic performance, teacher supervision, teaching aids and texts, and adequate physical space.

2.2.1 Historical Context of Education in Brazil

Education in Brazil was one of the historical moments that was marked by technological, social and political advances, preserving a people's memory.

With this, it (education) is considered a "bridge", making it possible for the individual to mutualise with the society in which they are inserted. In this way, it allows man to create patterns of behaviour, while at the same time being able to share new knowledge and new sciences (DINO, 2017).

According to Lopes (2013, p.14):

In Brazil, this collective process began with the colonisation of Brazil by Portugal through the Jesuits who, in addition to the customs and religiosity belonging to European culture, also brought the pedagogical methods that began the Brazilian educational system. Over the centuries, however, this educational system has undergone many changes and modifications.

This milestone in the history of education in Brazil has inspired the educational process to this day. It is known that education has gone through various phases and divisions, but Lopes (2002), among other authors, explains it as being divided into three major phases: colonial education, republican education and contemporary education, which will be studied further in the following sections.

2.2.1.1 Colonial Education

According to Aranha (2005), education in Brazil began with indigenous apprenticeships, which taught children the practices of planting, cooking and other activities in order to function optimally in the villages. They were taught to survive and live together in society.

The aforementioned author goes on to say that in 1549 the Jesuit priests arrived in Brazil and created the first Brazilian school, in Salvador. They were led by Father Manoel de Nóbrega, and were educated for 210 years by these teachers. With this educational model, they left their mark on Brazilian culture.

Sangenis (2004, p.93) explains:

> In fact, the Jesuits undertook significant missionary and evangelising work in Brazil, especially using new methodologies, of which school education was one of the most powerful and effective. When it came to school education, the Jesuits knew how to build their hegemony.

One of the Jesuits' pedagogical methods was the Ratio Studiorum [1] , in order to command functions, activity methods and assessments in the schools. The aim of these first teachers in Brazil was to get the Indians to abandon their beliefs. This educational model lasted until mid-1759 when, during the reign of Dom José I, the Prime Minister and future Marquis of Pombal instructed him to expel them on the grounds that they were "rebels, traitors, adversaries and aggressors" of their kingdoms (ALVES, 2012).

2.2.1.2 Republican Education

Education was reduced to almost nothing shortly after the expulsion of the Jesuit priests. According to Piletti and Piletti (2012), teachers were poorly trained and paid, so the system was "destroyed" and nothing was done to replace and/or organise it. It was only with the arrival of the Royal Family in Brazil from 1808 to 1821 that there were some changes in education, but only for the Portuguese Court. It remained abandoned until the Proclamation of the Republic in 1889.

Aranha (2005, p. 152) describes how the attributions of the Crown and the provinces were distributed:

> However, the coup de grâce that really damaged Brazilian education came from an amendment to the Constitution, the Additional Act of 1834. This reform decentralised education, assigning the Crown the task of promoting and regulating higher education, while the provinces (future states) were assigned elementary and secondary schools. In this way, the education of the elite was the responsibility of the central power and that of the people

---

[1] The Plan and Organisation of Studies of the Society of Jesus is a kind of collection, based on experiences at the Roman College, to which pedagogical observations from various other colleges have been added, the aim of which was to quickly instruct all Jesuit teachers on the nature, extent and obligations of their position.

Later, in the First Republic, from 1889 to 1929, Brazilian education once again suffered as a result of the switch from literary to scientific mastery. In the Second Republic, from 1930 to 1936, Brazil began to lack a labour force, thus initiating investment in Brazilian education. The period of the New Republic, from 1946 to 1963, was marked by debates on the Law of Guidelines and Bases - LDB (1961) (ALVES, 2012).

The aforementioned author goes on to emphasise one of the key events at the end of the Empire and the beginning of the Republic in Brazil, which was the end of slavery and the start of mass immigration of European peoples. This process, according to the writer, led to a shift from slave labour to wage labour in the countryside and, in some areas, in the city. Then came the Industrial Revolution, which demanded skilled labour and brought more changes to Brazilian education.

This republican period was marked by major political changes in Brazil. Various reforms were carried out at state and then national level. Some changes were of great importance, such as the creation of the National Commercial Apprenticeship Service - SENAC; the Magna Carta (1946); the Federal Education Council and the National Education Plan (1962) (ARANHA, 2005).

2.2.1.3 Contemporary education

Education in this period went through moments of regression, one of which was the military coup in 1964, a period in which many students and teachers were sacked, injured and/or imprisoned, and even killed, in clashes with the police who invaded and took control of the universities. As a result, education at that time was more political than pedagogical (ROMANELLI, 1991).

According to the author, it was during the military regime that Law 5.692, the National Education Guidelines and Bases Law - LDB, was instituted in 1971. The most striking feature of this law was its attempt to give education a vocational focus. The aim was to offer work opportunities to those who were unable to enter university.

The history of education since its inception has influenced and still influences the education that is still practised in Brazil. Education is a process that is always evolving. There has been a significant drop in illiteracy and a significant increase in the number of students in higher education (ALVES, 2012).

These changes came about, first of all, as a result of the Brazilian Federal Constitution's (1988) higher right to education. Article 205 of this law states that:

> Education, the right of all and the duty of the state and the family, will be promoted and encouraged with the collaboration of society, with a view to the full development of the person, their preparation for the exercise of citizenship and their qualification for work.

It was after the military period that a bill was sent to the Chamber of Deputies for the New Law of Guidelines and Bases - LDB, which was approved in 1996. Article 1 of Law 9.394/96 defines education as "the formative processes that develop in family life, in human coexistence, at work, in educational and research institutions, in social movements and civil society organisations and in cultural manifestations".

Subsequently, according to Aranha (2005), the National Curriculum Parameters - PCNs - were created, instituted as National Curriculum Guidelines through CEB Resolution No. 3 of 26 June 1998. These booklets, divided into related areas of teaching, were drawn up by the Federal Government to guide both public and private education in the country.

More recently, the National Education Plan - PNE (2010) was created, establishing goals for the ten-year period 2011-2020. According to its first article, it aims to "[...]

nationally articulate education systems in a collaborative regime and define guidelines, objectives, goals and their respective implementation strategies [...]" for education in Brazil. This was in order to fulfil Article 214 of the 1988 Constitution, which states:

> The law will establish the national education plan, of ten-year duration, with the aim of articulating the national education system in a system of collaboration and defining guidelines, objectives, goals and implementation strategies to ensure the maintenance and development of education at its various levels, stages and modalities through integrated actions by the public authorities of the different federative spheres that lead to:
> I - eradicating illiteracy;
> II - universalisation of school attendance;
> III - improving the quality of teaching;
> IV - training for work;
> V - the humanistic, scientific and technological promotion of the country.
> VI - setting a target for the application of public resources to education as a proportion of gross domestic product.

According to Alves (2012), change is part of education and is necessary because society is also multilevelled. We are probably close to a new breakthrough. And it is to be hoped that it will come with proposals unrelated to the European model of education, creating new solutions that respect Brazilian characteristics. One of the changes mentioned by the author is participatory management by the entire school community.

2.2.2 The Structure of Education in Brazil

In order to address issues related to school management, it is understood that it is first necessary to explain the structure of the workplace of the professional who works in this organisation.

The organisation of Brazilian education is separated into the Union, the States, the Federal District and the Municipalities. The bodies responsible for education at federal level are the National Education Council and the Ministry of Education (MEC); the State Education Secretary (SEE); the Regional Education Directorate (DRE) and the State Education Council (CEE) are responsible at state level (LOPES, 2013).

Brazilian school education is made up of Early Childhood Education, Primary Education, Secondary Education and Higher Education. There are other modalities besides those mentioned above: Youth and Adult Education (aimed at people who are returning to school after becoming adults); Professional or Technical Education; Special Education (aimed at people with disabilities) and Distance Education - EAD (education offered online rather than face-to-face). (VARGAS, 2013).

According to Vargas (2013), basic education consists of three stages: Early Childhood Education (0 to 5 years), Primary Education (6 to 14 years) and Secondary Education (15 to 17 years).

Technical education is education at secondary level, carried out in secondary schools or other institutions that award academic degrees or professional diplomas. There is also indigenous and quilombola education, which is offered in rural areas as basic education. In addition, Environmental Education is also considered to be an education, but it does not fit into a teaching modality, but is transversal within the others. Figure 2 shows that the items in yellow correspond to Basic Education and those in blue correspond to Undergraduate and Postgraduate programmes, including Masters and Doctorates.

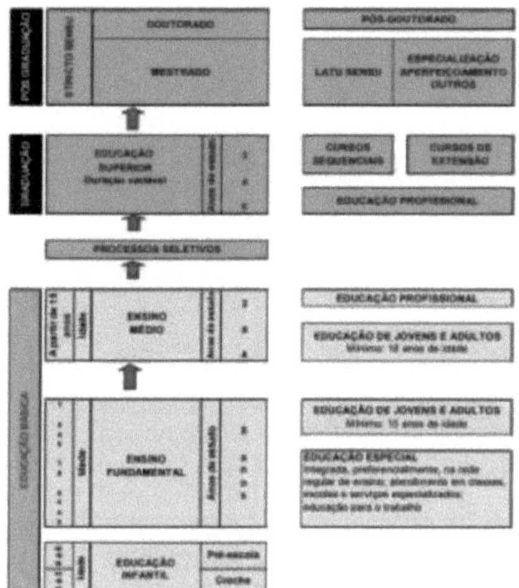

Figure 1 - Organisation and Structure of Brazilian Education
Source: National Education System of Brazil (2002).

According to Brazil's National Education System (2002), each educational institution, whether basic or higher, defines its own management model. They can adapt it to their economic, social and cultural needs, as well as taking into account the characteristics of their region.

2.2.2.1 Early childhood education

According to the Department of Basic Education, via the Ministry of Education's website (MEC, 2014), early childhood education caters for children between the ages of zero and three in crèches or Municipal Early Childhood Education Centres (CMEIs), and children between the ages of four and five in pre-schools. This is the first stage of education and is provided by public or public schools on a full or part-time basis.

Children in Early Childhood Education are not obliged to be enrolled, but the municipality must ensure that these children attend educational institutions. It is the government's obligation to provide this modality to everyone without distinction (MEC, 2014).

The document drawn up by the MEC (2013) in partnership with the General Coordination of Early Childhood Education "Frequently asked questions about Early Childhood Education" explains that in Early Childhood Education children develop autonomy by working in a playful way and through games, inserting the child into the teaching process.

According to INEP - Instituto Nacional de Estudos e Pesquisas Educacionais Anísio Teixeira (2016) the enrolment rate in Brazilian Early Childhood Education increases considerably every year. This is shown in Table 1.

Table 1 - Enrolment in Early Childhood Education from 2011 to 2016

YEAR	ENROLMENT IN EARLY CHILDHOOD EDUCATION		
	SCHOOL	PRE-SCHOOL	TOTAL
2011	2.298.707	4.681.345	6.980.052
2012	2.540.791	4.754.721	7.295.512
2013	2.730.119	4.860.481	7.590.600
2014	2.891.976	4.964.015	7.855.991
2015	3.043.548	4.916.525	7.960.073

| 2016 | 3.233.739 | 5.034.353 | 8.268.092 |

Source: Prepared by the authors (2017) based on the INEP School Census (2016).

Looking at the data in Table 1, we can see an increase in pre-school enrolment from 4,681,345 in 2011 to 5,034,353 in 2016. Table 1 also shows that in 2011 there were 2,298,707 children enrolled in crèches, while in 2016 this figure rose to 3,233,739.

With this expansion in enrolment, there is a notable need for new establishments for this age group. According to MEC (2013, p. 23), one of the projects created for this is "Brasil Carinhoso", which aims to "[...] provide financial support to expand the supply of early childhood education in new classes.".

2.2.2.2 Elementary School

Primary education is compulsory, so the state and the municipality must fulfil their obligations to offer this nine-year course universally and free of charge. It was made compulsory for children from the age of six by Law No. 11,114 of 16 May 2005, which amended the Law of Guidelines and Bases - LDB (1996) with the aim of making it compulsory to start primary school at the age of six.

With the increase in children's time in primary school, it was necessary to improve the quality of literacy training. To this end, it was established that in this modality, the student will have mastery of writing, reading, calculations and text production. They will also be able to understand the social, natural and political environment, basic social and family values and have knowledge of a foreign language (MEC, 2014).

Saviani (2007) believes that it is in primary school that people learn all the theory, all the philosophical and sociological concepts that will later be applied in practice in secondary school. For the author, this should be offered with the aim of transforming production relations in a democratic way.

Enrolment in primary education (1st to 9th grades) is much more popular than in early childhood education (Table 1) and secondary education (TABLE 2), as can be seen in Table 2 below. However, there was a considerable drop in enrolment between 2011 and 2016. According to INEP (2016), the main reason for this drop was the decrease in the six-year-old population.

Table 2 - Primary school enrolment from 2011 to 2016

| YEAR | PRIMARY SCHOOL ENROLMENT | | |
	BEGINNING YEARS	FINAL YEARS	TOTAL
2011	16.360.770	13.997.870	30.358.640
2012	16.016.030	13.686.468	29.702.498
2013	15.764.926	13.304.355	29.069.281
2014	15.699.483	12.760.184	28.459.667
2015	15.463.187	12.362.151	27.825.338
2016	15.346.008	12.242.897	27.588.905

Source: Prepared by the authors (2017) based on the INEP School Census (2016).

Another relevant piece of information is that the municipal network, with 10.4 million pupils, accounts for 68 per cent of the total number of registrations in the early years and groups together 82.9 per cent of pupils in the public network.

2.2.2.3 Secondary education

According to LDB 9.394/96 (BRASIL, 1996), in its article 35, the purpose of secondary education is to:

I - the consolidation and deepening of the knowledge acquired in primary education, enabling further study;
II - the basic preparation for work and citizenship of the student, to continue learning, so as to be able to adapt flexibly to new conditions of occupation or further training;
III - the development of the student as a human being, including ethical training and the development of intellectual autonomy and critical thinking;
IV - an understanding of the scientific and technological foundations of production processes, relating theory to practice in the teaching of each subject.

Secondary education is considered a basic stage in the educational process and is necessary for the formation of the individual. It lasts three years and

last stage of basic education. It is considered a foundation for students before they enter higher education (MEC, 2014).

According to INEP (2016), the private network has around one million students (12.5 per cent), which has grown by 4.5 per cent in eight years. The state network accounts for 84.8 per cent of enrolments, with 96.9 per cent of students in the public network.

Table 3 - Secondary school enrolments from 2011 to 2016

YEAR	SECONDARY SCHOOL ENROLMENTS
2011	8.400.689
2012	8.376.852
2013	8.312.815
2014	8.300.189
2015	8.074.881
2016	8.131.988

Source: Prepared by the authors (2017) based on the INEP School Census (2016).

In secondary education, the National Curriculum Parameters (PCNs) are used to help the school team, assisting in the development of practices, lesson planning and the development of the school, helping the professionals who work in this phase of education. These Cadernos (PCNs) were created in 1996, after the LDB (1996) and are aimed above all at structuring and restructuring school curricula throughout Brazil, being compulsory for the public network and optional for private institutions.

2.2.2.4 Higher Education

Higher education is offered by private and public institutions in Brazil. Students choose one of three types of degree: bachelor's, licentiate or technological. Higher education institutions also offer postgraduate courses, Masters and Doctorates.

The role of HEIs is to train graduates in various areas of activity, offering students practical research and scientific investigation, and activities to intervene in society that will be developed over the course of their university education. Universities need to be accredited by the MEC in order to operate fully.

Chapter V of the LDB (1996) clarifies the functions of higher education in articles 43 to 57. It also clarifies that in order to enter an HEI, students must go through a selection process, one of the most commonly used being the entrance exam. Undergraduate programmes can vary in length from 3 to 6 years.

It is worth emphasising that higher education is not the focus of this study, only the management used in basic education. In view of this, the following chapters look at the definition and function of management in schools.

2.2.3 Management Concepts

The word "management" comes from the Latin word "gestio", expressing the action of administering, leading, governing. The term management is related to administration, leading an organisation to achieve its objectives. In the Portuguese language dictionary, it is defined as "Efeito ou ato de gerir" (Effect or act of managing) (FERREIRA, 2009, p. 274). On the same page, the word "gerir" is defined as "To have management over, to administer, to direct, to manage".

Oliveira, Perez and Silva (2002, p. 136) define management as:

> The term management derives from the Latin gestione and means to manage, administration. To administer is to plan, organise, direct and control resources in order to achieve a certain goal. To manage is to make things happen and lead the organisation towards its goals. Therefore, management is the act of leading in order to achieve the desired results.

Management is a job in which people try to achieve their goals in order to achieve their objectives. And these goals are an integral part of the decision that is the basis of the administrative act. The act of managing would be incomplete without the decisions and functions of planning, organising, leading and executing, and in this way management is able to achieve its goals (DIAS, 2002).

It can therefore be understood from the aforementioned author's ideas that management, as such, involves both a set of procedures that are carried out to resolve an issue or realise a project and the act of carrying out actions, guiding towards the achievement of the proposed goals and objectives.

Dias (2002, p. 10-11) argues that there is a difference between administration and management. For him, administration is "planning, organising, directing and controlling people to achieve an organisation's objectives efficiently and effectively", while management is "using all the functions and knowledge necessary to achieve an organisation's objectives efficiently and effectively through people".

For these management processes to be more successful, they need to be linked to good administration procedures. Therefore, Dias (2002) emphasises that in order to achieve good results, they (management and administration) must go hand in hand, one complementing the other.

2.2.3.1 Taylorism and School Administration

Frederic Winslow Taylor (1856-1915) is considered the "father" of Scientific Management, influencing management concepts to this day. With a degree in engineering, he worked for many years as the manager of various factories, enabling him to carry out a study to improve the development of employee productivity (SILVA, 2011).

According to the aforementioned author, to this end, he set out objectives for good management, encouraging competition between workers, dividing up the organisation and reducing production costs. He also advocated fairer wages for labourers, so that higher wages would be paid to those who worked harder and better.

Taylor (1990, p. 43) defines that there is a type of worker suited to a specific function.

> One type of man is needed to plan and a different one to carry out the work. [...] in almost all the mechanical arts, the science which governs the operations of labour is so vast and complex that the best worker adapted to his function is incapable of understanding it, either from lack of study or from insufficient mental capacity.

Taylor's method envisaged the separation of manual and intellectual labour. For him, each worker was a science, possessing professional knowledge and experience, knowing how to choose the work solutions presented through creativity, attached to their traditions, they needed to be studied, classified and systematised (SILVA, 2011).

Taylor (1990) developed four basic principles that were widely passed on in the industrial sector. These are: 1st principle: Limit the knowledge of the workers by studying the time used for each task with chronometers introduced into the workshops. 2nd principle: Select, train, perfect and teach the worker. Principle 3: Establishing a good relationship between the factory organisation and the workers. Principle 4: Maintaining the separation of labour and responsibilities between workers and management, centring power on management, thus excluding producers.

According to Silva (2011), the Taylorist system highlighted two characteristics: 1) The emergence of the analyst function and the particularisation of salaries. 2) The competition between workers and the production of each one with their different way of working.

Marques (2007) explains that the fundamental principles of Taylor's Scientific Management (1990) determine principles of educational policy that the school should consider as a body in an attempt to meet the needs of scientific work. Thus, in the author's ideas, work (management) in the school should:

a) Making use of the knowledge of the connections between people to be able to determine what their objectives might be is a useful methodology;
b) The administration determines what everyone has to do, and it's up to them to draw up timetables, curricula, textbooks, etc., and for the rest of us just to carry out the school planning;
c) With the separation for the execution of the work, it is essential that everyone involved in the project is involved in all stages of the work;
d) At school, work needs to be divided up, explaining what is to be taught, how it is to be taught and how long it is to be taught.

It can be noted that this comparison of the principles of scientific management activities with school administration shows the modification of the Taylorist division of labour by team or individual activities requiring autonomy, initiative and also the ability to solve problems.

For Silva (211), this is the challenge of management, and from these actions it can be seen that the changes are significant not only for society in general, but for our lives on a daily basis. Marques (2007) opposes the competitiveness proposed by Taylor, because according to him, competitiveness must be removed from the school environment, excluding forms of oppression, discrimination, violence and exclusion.

2.2.3.2 Types of management

According to Maximiano (2006), management can be summed up as the control of a situation, strategy and/or people within an organisation. It also refers to the process of determination, guiding the right path to follow in order to realise its objectives. To do this, the manager uses a series of decisions, leadership, motivation, evaluation and analysis.

There are various management models, according to Kwasnicka (2003) these three are the main ones:

a) Traditional management: Prevalent until the 1930s, it was linked to hierarchy, lacked autonomy and creative involvement in work, and had a bureaucratic, mechanistic character, coming from the legacy of Fayol and Taylor.
b) Modern management: In this model, the employee is seen as a human being who has feelings, needs and emotions, beginning in the late 1930s and continuing until the 1960s, with a behavioural, systematic character, greatly influenced by the behavioural sciences.
c) Contemporary management: beginning in the 1960s and continuing until the 1980s, this period was characterised by an indeterminate and organised approach. Institutions had to adapt to new labour market conditions and seek out new technologies. There were more concerns than just profit (FIGURE 3).

In contemporary management, there is dynamism among administrators, and adaptations and innovations are necessary. This requires new managers with experience in new technologies, but Kwasnicka (2003) believes that the inclusion of these newly trained professionals creates a conflict with older managers. This is due to the differences in ideas between the new (dynamism and new technologies) and the old (experience). The author emphasises, therefore, that both have a lot to learn from each other and that they should get on well together, even though they have different personalities and skills.

It can be seen that the contemporary management model in Figure 3 is a systemic and behavioural model. It focuses on people and the organisational environment, considering the organisation to be an open system that interacts (in various ways) with the environment.

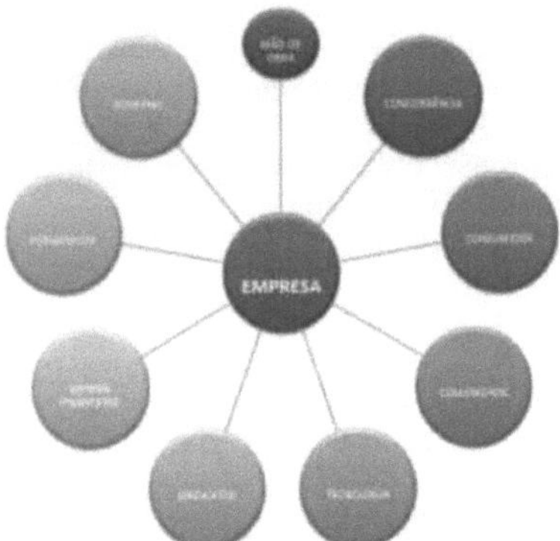

Figure 2 - Contemporary Management Model
Source: Organised by the authors (2017) according to Kwasnicka's concepts (2003).

There are currently other models based on these three. Examples include Participative Management, Competence Management, Knowledge Management, Organisational Culture Management, Educational Management and School Management. The last two are the focus of this study and are discussed more clearly in the following chapter.

2.2.3.3 Educational Management and School Management

Educational management is based on the organisation of federal, state and municipal education systems and their obligations. In addition, according to Santos (2008), there are also various ways of dealing with the particularities that determine the norms, executing and deliberating in the education sector.

Luck (2007, p. 33-34) defines educational management as a relationship of the whole and not of the parts, as can be seen in his lecture:

> Educational management is an expression that has gained prominence in the literature and acceptance in the educational context, especially since the 1990s, and has become a common concept in the discourse guiding the actions of education systems and schools. [...] The concept of management is the result of a new understanding of how organisations are run, which takes into account the whole in relation to the parts and the parts in relation to each other, in order to promote greater effectiveness of the whole.

It is therefore understood that each system has an important role to play in the educational context. Therefore, the states and the Federal District have the role of drawing up and executing educational plans and the municipalities are responsible for organising, maintaining and executing them through integration with the federal and state educational plans (LIBÂNEO, 2008).

According to Santos (2008), school management is different from educational management. The author believes that educational management is perceived through the initiatives drawn up by the education system, while school management is situated within the school, promoting teaching and learning for all, without deprivation.

Santos (2008) adds that it is up to each school to draw up and implement its own pedagogical proposal, assemble its staff, manage financial and material resources, pay attention to the teaching of each student, provide teaching methods and ensure that there is a process of integration with students, families and the community. This will therefore fall to school management.

Educational management has emerged to complement school management. Mentioned in Law 9.394/96 (BRASIL, 1996), schools have the autonomy to cater for the particularities of each student, while respecting the norms of the education system.

In Brazil, educational management is determined by guidelines that are mentioned in the country's law, specifying the participatory and progressive model of school administration, characterising it as educational management and not just school management (LUCK, 2007).

The difference, therefore, between educational management and school management is that the former is at the macro level (where the higher bodies of education systems and public policies are located) and the latter at the micro level (where schools and the work carried out in them are located).

Luck (2007, p. 55) explains educational management as follows:

> The concept of educational management, therefore, presupposes a different understanding of reality, of the elements involved in an action and of the people themselves in their context; it encompasses a series of conceptions, focusing on social interactivity, not considered by the concept of administration, and therefore surpassing it.

Santos (2008) emphasises that despite this distinction, they are interlinked by articulating their actions in pursuit of the same objectives. Both involve community participation, but the latter is more effective and more visible, for example in school councils.

2.2.4 School management

School management encompasses all of the institution's practices. The manager is therefore responsible for organising and developing the school, drawing up, executing and coordinating projects and plans. According to Paro (2003), for the functions to be carried out successfully, management can be categorised into three areas:

a) Pedagogical School Management: determines teaching objectives, setting them according to the profile of the students, drawing up curriculum content, proposing targets to be met, monitoring and evaluating the performance of the teachers, management team and students;

b) Administrative School Management: related to institutional and physical management. The institutional part is the activities of the school secretariat, the rights and duties and also the school regulations, and the physical part consists of the institution's property and materials;

c) Human Resources Management: refers to the relationship that the school has with the students' parents, the students, teachers, the administration and also the community, ensuring that the institution runs smoothly, resolving problems and issues that concern people's relationships.

These three areas need to work together to keep the educational process organised. Other authors such as Sangenis (2004) add two more distinctions: School Financial Management, Communication Management and Time Management and Process Efficiency, which are itemised in Figure 4 below:

Figure 3 - The six pillars of school management
Source: Gestão Escolar Digital magazine (2011)

It can therefore be concluded that school management is divided into 6 main pillars that seek administrative, financial and pedagogical autonomy and the optimisation of time and processes in regular educational institutions and courses. These pillars are interdependent and the proper functioning of these spheres is vital for the institution. Therefore, as Libâneo (2008) states, managers must dedicate themselves with commitment to different areas of activity in order to succeed in their role and obtain good results, such as those described in Figure 5.

The LDB (1996) in its Title IV, on the organisation of National Education, in Article 13, describes that the teacher must participate in the individual and collective planning carried out in schools:

> Art. 13: Teachers will be responsible for:
> I - take part in drawing up the school's pedagogical proposal;
> II - draw up and fulfil a work plan, in accordance with the educational establishment's pedagogical proposal; [...]
> V - [...] participate fully in periods dedicated to planning, evaluation and professional development;
> VI - collaborate with the school's liaison activities with families and the community.

According to Padilha (2001), planning is one of the main obligations of schools. According to the author, it becomes effective when everyone (parents, teachers, students, managers and the school community) participates in the planning process, and can be put into practice through social actions, in order to involve the school in society and vice versa. This was already provided for in Article 14 of the LDB (1996): "II - participation of the school and local communities in school councils or equivalent.".

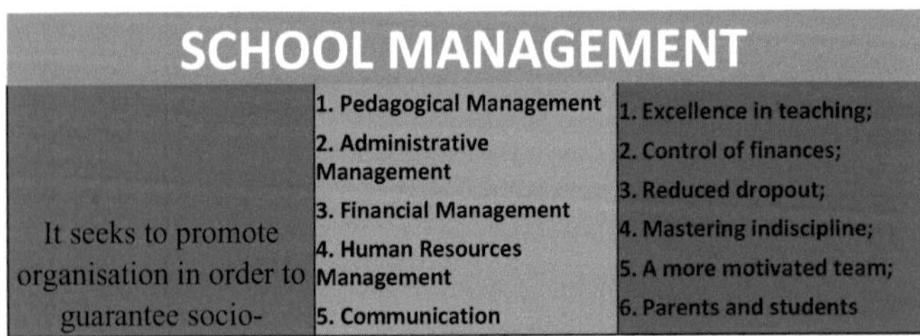

SCHOOL MANAGEMENT		
It seeks to promote organisation in order to guarantee socio-	1. Pedagogical Management	1. Excellence in teaching;
	2. Administrative Management	2. Control of finances;
	3. Financial Management	3. Reduced dropout;
	4. Human Resources Management	4. Mastering indiscipline;
	5. Communication	5. A more motivated team;
		6. Parents and students

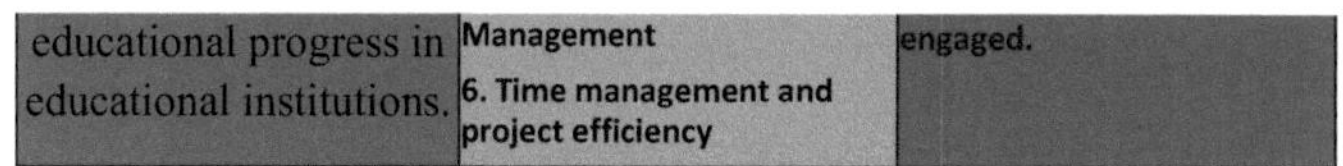

Figure 4 - Definition, Types and Results of School Management
Source: Organised by the authors (2017) based on data from Revista Gestão Escolar (2011).

For institutions to function, a process of school organisation and development must take place. According to Libâneo (2005), this system is made up of four functions: planning, organisation, management and evaluation.

Padilha (2001, p. 63) defines school planning as:

> Let's remember that making educational and school plans means carrying out an engaged, intentional, scientific, political and ideological activity that is free from neutrality. Planning, in a broad sense, is a process that aims to provide answers to a problem, by establishing ends and means that aim to overcome it, to achieve previously foreseen objectives, necessarily thinking about and foreseeing the future, but without disregarding the conditions of the present and the experiences of the past, taking into account the contexts and the philosophical, cultural, economic and political assumptions of those who plan and those with whom they plan.

Planning is made up of procedures and actions, thus deciding which activities will be carried out and the objective of each one. Pascoal (2014) lists what should be considered when drawing up the school's annual plan, indicating the objectives and the means used to carry them out.

a) Welcoming new teachers;
b) Exchange of experiences between teachers and managers;
c) Presentation and analysis of the previous year's results;
d) Setting goals and objectives;
e) Presentation of the school calendar, according to the one provided by the Department of Education;
f) Revision of the Political-Pedagogical Project and creation of action plans;
g) Definition of the course timetable;
h) Class division;
i) Organisation of rooms and materials;
j) Welcoming the students;
k) Pedagogical planning, taking into account the previous year's assessment and the distribution of teaching and learning content.

The aforementioned author emphasises that meeting agendas are flexible and can be altered according to the needs of each institution and the participants. A lack of planning at school will jeopardise the commitment to the educational process.

Planning is the simple fact of thinking before carrying out an action. Without planning, the individual does not carry out their activity, thus characterising the act of thinking and acting as a form of planning (HONORATO, 2012).

The organisation of work is related to physical, material and financial resources and the ability to use these resources for work. The general organisation of the school is related to materials, physical and financial conditions, assistance to teachers, cleaning, timetables, administrative services, enrolment, rules, distribution of pupils in classes, contact with pupils' parents and society, etc. Management and coordination, on the other hand, are represented by the activities carried out by the management team, including monitoring work, carrying out collective work and assessing the team's performance (ARAÚJO, 2000).

According to Libâneo (2005) directing and coordinating means taking responsibility for making the school run smoothly, carrying out collective work. It is the role of the school manager to coordinate the activities of the various sectors of the school, carrying out a participatory process by making decisions to keep the school environment organised.

Luckesi (1992, p. 119) criticises the practice of planning in Brazilian schools:

[...] the practice of planning in our country, especially in education, has been conducted as if it were a neutral, uncompromising activity. [...] however, there is little or no discussion about the real social and political significance of the action being planned. There is no question of the social determinants that underlie the problem to be tackled, nor is there any discussion of the possible political and social consequences that will result from the implementation of the project in question.

It is essential, therefore, that school managers have training, which implies a good planning process for changes and innovations in the school. The training of this professional consists of higher education and continuing education courses, so it is up to the education system to train these professionals by promoting training and preparation courses for the school manager, with the task of planning, monitoring and programming pedagogical projects in order to promote the integration of the school with the community, mobilising the professionals included in education while maintaining communication and dialogue between them. (LUPORINI; MARTINIAK; MAROCHI, 2011).

In this training, the manager will realise that evaluation is essential in school organisation and management. Because it (evaluation) allows them to highlight the difficulties in practice between planning and carrying out the work, seeking to correct and improve their mistakes and difficulties encountered in the project. (LUCKESI, 1992).

In order for the manager to collect and evaluate information about the functioning of the institution, he or she must monitor the activities inside the classrooms, during breaks, meetings, teachers' conversations with students' parents, and meetings with the administrative and pedagogical staff. This action on the part of the manager will greatly improve the quality of teaching and the school's profile, providing support and fixing some of the flaws during this process (LUPORINI; MARTINIAK; MAROCHI, 2011).

The aforementioned authors emphasise that evaluation is important because it leads to an analysis of the results collected by the manager, taking the necessary measures to solve the problems encountered. It is also necessary for institutions to have a school council, administrative area, management, pedagogical sector and teaching staff.

Werle (2003) describes these sectors as:

a) The School Council: represented by issues of state and municipal legislation and the school regulations, administrative, pedagogical and financial aspects, with the function of democratising its power relations.

b) Administrative Sector: responsible for the school's functions, cleaning services, secretarial services and customer service.

c) Management: managing and organising the school's activities, always helping the teachers and students.

d) The Pedagogical Sector: activities carried out by the pedagogical coordinator with functions that vary according to state or municipal legislation.

e) The Teaching Staff: A group of teachers whose job it is to carry out the teaching-learning process for the students.

While planning is the act by which we decide what to build, assessment is the critical act that helps us to check how we are building our project. Luckesi (1992, p. 125) adds that "Evaluation crosses the act of planning and execution; that is why it contributes throughout the course of the planned action [...] it is a tool that human beings cannot get rid of. It is part of their way of acting

2.2.4.1 Training and the Choice of School Manager

Good training for managers to work in the field of education is essential for dynamic and well-organised action. Schools are characterised by initiatives, conflicts and challenges and school management needs to be recognised and taken seriously. Luporini, Martiniak and

Marochi (2011) believe that management training has been inadequate and undefined.

In this field, experience alone is not enough. In this respect, Santos (2008, p. 12) defines the profile of this manager as "Modernity demands managers who are more dynamic, creative and capable of interpreting the demands of each moment and of establishing more appropriate working conditions in the school".

As a result, there are many issues that have caused concerns, worries and questions in which the school manager becomes responsible for actions, conditions, changes and modifications in the organisation of the school.

Article 61 of the LDB (1996) emphasises that basic education schools need to be led by trained professionals, promoting democracy through professionalism and competence. And Article 64 of the same law states:

> The training of education professionals for administration, planning, inspection, supervision and educational guidance for basic education will be carried out in undergraduate pedagogy courses or in postgraduate courses, at the discretion of the institution, guaranteeing a common national basis for this training.

It should be noted that the law requires a degree in pedagogy or a postgraduate course. There are two obstacles in the system, identified by Paro (2004): the first is that the Pedagogy course does not offer (in full) training that is equivalent to performing the job, and the second is that it is not specified which postgraduate course the manager must take.

The process of comprehensive and interdisciplinary training encourages school work, strengthening autonomy through organised, humane and democratic work carried out collectively. It develops educational policy with commitment and responsibility, showing that teaching and learning have important purposes in the school environment.

Padilha (1998) says that the choice of headteacher in Brazil is made through the traditional "appointment" by the government, but the author believes that this is not a "democratic" way. In his opinion, this choice should come from a list nominated by the school community; through tests and/or qualifications; or through the election of candidates chosen by the School Council, in order to avoid possible clientelism or influence from the executive.

According to Padilha (1998, p.70) apud Paro (1998) explains that of all the possibilities mentioned above, "Election is the most democratic form, since appointment, even with some community participation, tends towards political-clientelist criteria."

The public competition for headmasters ends up consolidating a divergence between the professional teacher and the professional manager. This is the warning given by Medeiros

(2003), who argues that this election is a "step backwards" in relation to the proposition that the administrative, pedagogical and financial dimensions are intrinsically intertwined in the teaching process. The author advocates a democratic election proposed and organised by the community in general and by the school community.

2.2.4.2 Associative and Democratic Organisations

Democratic management is also established in the Federal Constitution (1988), in Article 206: "VI - democratic management of public education, in the form of the law" and later in the LDB (1996), Article 3: "VIII - democratic management of public education, in the form of this Law and the legislation of the education systems".

The aim of democratic management is to develop a space in the school that implies the construction of a public policy, with the effective participation of headmasters, students, teachers, the community and parents in a harmonious way. Even in the 1990s, Lawler (1990) argued that this management model brings benefits, such as the creation of the curriculum by the school itself, causing the training of education professionals to remain permanent.

According to the MEC Portal, the School Development Plan (PDE) was launched as a management tool that helps schools do their job better. It helps to focus its energy, ensure that its staff work towards the same goals and evaluate and adapt its direction in response to a constantly changing environment.

The PDE (BRASIL, 2006a, p. 13) explains that the School Development Plan is often confused with the pedagogical proposal. It explains: "The PDE sees the school as a whole from a strategic perspective, not just from a pedagogical perspective." To carry it out, five steps need to be taken:

a) STEP 1 - Preparation for and of the PDE
b) STEP 2 - Situational Analysis
c) STEP 3 - Defining the Strategic Vision and the Strategic Support Plan
d) STAGE 4 - Execution, Monitoring and Evaluation
e) STEP 5 - Monitoring and Evaluation

For the PDE to be carried out successfully, it requires the dedication of the leadership, especially the manager, because it is he who will lead the process in which it will be drawn up and inserted with commitment to the plan, providing support so that the stages are successfully completed. It is therefore a tool to be used to plan strategies and school activities with the aim of making the process more useful for the school and the community (BRASIL, 2006a).

The school's Political Pedagogical Project (PPP) aims to make the school more useful by making it reflect on what is to be taught, how it is to be taught and how the student is to be assessed. It also defines the school's social, cultural and educational role. It is therefore up to the headteacher (together with the pedagogical team) to draw up and incorporate this pedagogical proposal, associating it with the PDE (VEIGA, 2003).

From this perspective, the project is "[...] a means of collective engagement to integrate dispersed actions, to create synergies in order to seek alternative solutions for different moments in the pedagogical-administrative work (VEIGA, 2000, p. 275).

The School Council or Collegiate is represented as the new phase of the public school, acting together with the school management, helping to face problems and make decisions in the pedagogical, financial and administrative space, its members being responsible for the task of education. Based on the LDB (1996), in its Article 14, Item II, establishing some principles of democratic education, showing the importance of the participation of the school community in school councils, to make decisions about the educational process.

Werle (2003, p. 102) explains what school councils are as follows:

> School councils take on life and material form in the articulations between the social actors that make them up; in the way parents, students, teachers, staff and management appropriate the council's space while building it in a dynamic and conflictive way.

It is the role of the School Council to participate in drawing up, monitoring and evaluating the implementation of the pedagogical proposal, evaluating the results of the learning process, suggesting ideas for improvement, coordinating elections for Principal and Vice-Principal, being responsible for the implementation and monitoring of the proposal, receiving reports on the performance of each student, monitoring the attendance of teachers and the administrative area, monitoring the school census. (WERLE, 2003).

It is important for the development of effective management that teachers, students and parents are encouraged to organise the exercise in order to lead responsibly. All council members need to be aware that participating in decisions makes it necessary to understand collective needs. The manager's role at this point is to organise, coordinate and encourage the school council (PADILHA, 2001).

The Council of Class Representatives and the Student Guild are bodies that represent the students of the school and are organised and run by the students. Their aim is to train student leaders in matters involving the organisation of teaching and the promotion of educational and sporting activities, as well as improving student practices. Therefore, the creation of these entities highlights democratisation within schools. It is up to managers to promote and encourage the establishment of these bodies (RAMOS, 2014).

Among these categories is the Class Council, which is held in the presence of teachers and students. It works in the same way as the school council and must be ready to receive suggestions from the school and the students. Libâneo (2005, p. 340) states that the school council has "consultative, deliberative and fiscal attributions in matters defined in state or municipal legislation and in the school regulations". It is therefore understood that this Council tends to help the manager in his work.

Aline Santana Martins apud Ramos (2014) stresses that it is up to this body to reflect on the pedagogical project, analysing the participation of all those involved in the learning process. The School Council is responsible for "innovating the perception of the class council, turning it into a process of institutional evaluation (RAMOS, 2014, 148).

Educational planning is the transformation of teachers' ideas into practice. The act of planning must be geared towards the student, seeking to improve the learning process. It is the school manager's responsibility to guide, observe and monitor the implementation of teachers' plans, with a view to adapting them to the school's reality. (BRASIL, 2006a)

In short, managers should be aware that they have an obligation to know, implement, coordinate and encourage the following school bodies: the School Development Plan; the Pedagogical Political Project; the School Council or Collegiate Body; the School Council; the Council of Class Representatives and the Student Guild; the Class Council; Educational Planning.

In order to coordinate all these segments, the school manager must practise democratic management, as mentioned above, and motivate everyone involved in the institution. Penna (2001) believes that motivated people are more productive, happier and have healthy relationships, making them successful. When there is no motivational cycle, they become frustrated, aggressive, dissatisfied, nervous, disinterested, pessimistic and insecure.

Lawler (1990, p. 139) explains that in order for work to be motivating "[...] individuals need to feel personally responsible for the outcome of the work, they need to do something that they feel is meaningful, and they need to receive feedback [2] on what has been achieved".

It is therefore understood that in order to carry out democratic and participatory management, managers need to be aware of the importance of working in groups, valuing their school staff, creating a favourable climate in the workplace, transforming moments of learning into moments of interaction and reflection, with harmonious relationships.

Improving the quality of teaching is related to autonomous management, considering content, method and the coexistence of participants in the teaching-learning process to be inseparable. The mere transmission of knowledge and the administration of the establishment are not enough. Today's managers must manage responsibly, motivating and interacting with the school community, keeping up to date and sharing knowledge.

---

[2] Information that the sender obtains from the receiver's reaction to their message, and which serves to evaluate the results of the transmission.

CHAPTER 3

METHODOLOGICAL FRAMEWORK

3.1 FOCUS AND TYPE OF INVESTMENT

The aim of this study was to survey the profile of managers (headmasters) of municipal schools in the city of Caldas Novas-GO.

According to Demo (2000), research varies according to its genres and, in practice, one type is mixed with another. That said, no type of research is self-sufficient. In this study, the aim was to use descriptive research, since the aim is to survey and describe the profile of the headteachers of municipal schools. Numerical data will also be used in this description, making it a mixed or qualitative-quantitative study.

3.2 TIME AND SPACE DELIMITATION

The data was collected from August 2016 to November 2016, a period that was deemed sufficient to carry out a detailed investigation of the data that was intended to be collected. The scope is restricted to the municipality of Caldas Novas, Goiás, Brazil, specifically the 14 municipal schools that the city currently has that cater for primary school students in the urban area.

3.3 POPULATION AND SAMPLE

All the headmasters (18) of the municipal schools in the city of Caldas Novas-GO. The total number of students in the municipality (12,000 students) and the total number of teachers (1,500 teachers).

Only the headmasters of municipal primary schools in the urban area will be included, thus excluding vice-principals, coordinators and secretaries. The sample will also include 10 teachers and 10 students chosen at random by the researcher from these same institutions.

3.4 .2 Sample to be used

14 headmasters from 14 municipal schools (elementary and urban) in the city of Caldas Novas-GO. In addition to the headmasters, 10 teachers and 10 students, selected at random by the researcher, also took part in the field research. This method was chosen so that there would be no management interference in the choice of participants.

3.6 HYPOTHESIS

The hypothesis is that the headmasters in office have no training in school management, which prevents them from carrying out truly democratic management.

3.7 DATA COLLECTION TECHNIQUES AND INSTRUMENTS

According to Lakatos and Marconi (2003), this phase of the research is carried out in order to gather prior information on the field of interest and involves collecting data from various sources.

The interview, according to Gil (2008), is very suitable as a data collection technique for obtaining information about what people know, believe, expect, feel or desire, intend to do, do or have done, as well as about their explanations or reasons for the preceding things

A semi-structured interview (APPENDIX A) was therefore carried out with the headmasters of the municipal schools in order to find out their profile and how their school management is being carried out.

According to Lakatos and Marconi (2003, p. 21) "[...] an ordered series of questions that must be answered in writing and without the presence of the interviewer".

Therefore, in addition to the interviews with the headmasters, a questionnaire (APPENDIX B) was administered to 10 teachers and 10 students (from each institution surveyed) in order to ascertain the effectiveness of the management used by the headmaster who took part in the field research.

3.8 SOURCES OF INFORMATION: PRIMARY AND SECONDARY

Our primary sources will be interviews with the headmasters of municipal schools in the city of Caldas Novas-GO, as well as a questionnaire administered to some of the teachers and students at these schools.

As secondary sources we will use books, articles, monographs, theses, texts available on the Internet, databases, newspapers, magazines, films, among others that deal with school management and the attributes of a head teacher.

3.9 HOW THE DATA COLLECTED WILL BE PROCESSED

The data collected from the interview with the headmasters was analysed using graphs and descriptive data. On the other hand, the data found through the application of the questionnaire to teachers and students was represented only through graphs, as it only contained closed questions.

3.10 ETHICAL CONSIDERATIONS

The interviewees' real names were not used to preserve their identity. To this end, enumerators (DIRECTOR 1) were used to refer to headmasters (DIRECTOR 1), teachers (TEACHER 2) and students (STUDENT 3), if necessary.

Only the names of the schools have been preserved to give a better idea of the scale of municipal education. When necessary, vague and broad terms will be used so as not to expose the image of the institution.

CHAPTER 4

ANALYTICAL FRAMEWORK

This chapter will present the results of the data collected from the interview with the managers (headmasters) of the municipal schools, as well as the questionnaire applied to the teachers and students of the institutions in the municipality of Caldas Novas, Goiás, Brazil.

As for the current population of teachers and students in the municipality, Table 4 shows the schools, neighbourhoods and number of teachers and students per institution. The data was provided by the Caldas Novas Municipal Department of Education and Leisure - SEMEL

Table 4 - Population of teachers and students per school

N°	MUNICIPAL SCHOOL	NEIGHBOURHOOD	Teachers (Quantity)	Students QQuaniity)
1	Mrs Abelina	Boa Vista Resort	14	222
2	Celina Belo	Holliday	10	439
3	Edith Ala	Breeze Park	38	861
4	EJA Youth/Adults	St Joseph		
5	Feliciano Ivo	Jardim Paraíso II	08	295
6	Felipe Marinho	Jequitimar	10	256
7	Geraldo Dias	Grupinho village		
8	Hélia Rodrigues	New Town		
9	Limírio Rosa	Holliday	10	408
10	Mather Isabel	St Joseph	22	565
11	Norbeto Odebrecht	M. das Águas Quentes	08	214
12	Orlando Rodrigues	Itaguaí II	16	481
13	Orozina Maria	Serrano Garden	18	481
14	Prof Zico Batista	Royal Park	22	700
15	Reginaldo Ríspole	Jardim Brasil	08	239
16	Santa Efigênia	Santa Efigênia	45	975
17	Valdir Arantes	University Sector	20	348
18	Waldomiro G. Souza	Sapé village		
	14 Municipal Schools (surveyed)		249	6.484

Source: Organised by the authors (2017) with data provided by SEMEL (2016)

It should be noted that schools 4, 7, 8 and 18 did not take part in this research. Number 4 also caters for adults, who are not the focus of this study. Numbers 7 and 18 are rural schools and are run differently from urban schools. And number 8 is a school for people with disabilities that doesn't have the same public or the same policy.

4.1 ANALYSIS OF THE QUESTIONNAIRE APPLIED TO TEACHERS AND STUDENTS

It is worth noting that the sample used in this research was 10 teachers and 10 students (chosen at random) in each school, totalling 140 teachers and 140 students from the municipal school system in the city of Caldas Novas. Both answered the questionnaire in Annex B, totalling 280 participants.

They were selected at random by the researcher herself in order to avoid management influence on the answers. The questionnaire was administered to students in the 2nd[a] phase of primary school (7th to 9th grades), in order to get more concrete and mature responses. The survey took place between August and October 2016.

A school was visited each week, in the afternoon and morning, so that teachers and students from the same school could be interviewed, but in different periods.

Both administrations provided a room for the researcher to gather the research participants and analyse the documents provided by the institution, as well as conducting the interview with the school management.

We tried to administer the questionnaire to 5 teachers and parents from the morning classes and 5 parents and teachers from the afternoon classes, in order to get a fairer and more homogeneous result.

There was no resistance to taking part in the research. We endeavoured to carry out the survey during the break, before or after the students' class period and the same period as the teachers' office hours, so as not to impede the smooth running and routine of the institution.

The questionnaire was administered by reading and signing the Informed Consent Form (Appendix D). Afterwards, the participant was given the 13-item questionnaire.

The first question asked was whether the headmaster "ensures that the teachers' activities are in line with the school's educational goals".

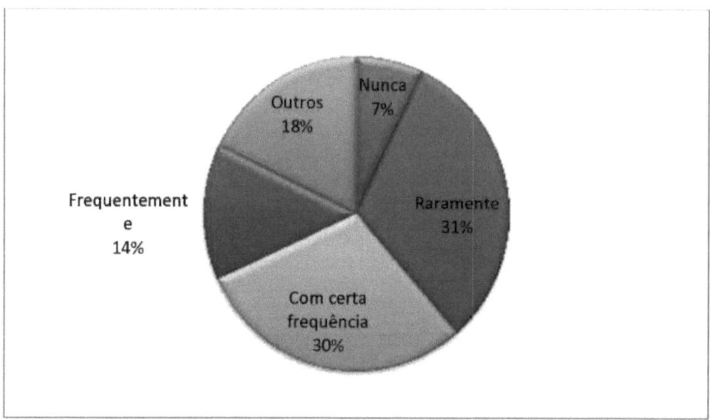

Graph 1 - Follows the teacher's activities
Source: Organised by the authors (2017)

Graph 1 shows that 31 per cent replied that they rarely follow the activities, 30 per cent replied that they follow them fairly often and 14 per cent said that they often do.

07% of teachers and students replied that the headmaster never monitors the activities carried out by teachers to check that they are in line with the school's educational goals.

Of particular note here is the "Other" option, which reached 18 per cent. In this case, most of the students who ticked this box said that they couldn't say that the coordinator monitored the activities carried out by the teachers.

Question 2 asked whether the headmaster "observes teaching in the classroom". Graph 2 shows that 55 per cent of respondents said that the headmaster rarely observes classroom teaching.

While 13 per cent said that this happens fairly often. Only 7% answered "often". A percentage of 25 per cent of respondents, totalling 69, including teachers and students, said that management "never" observes classroom teaching.

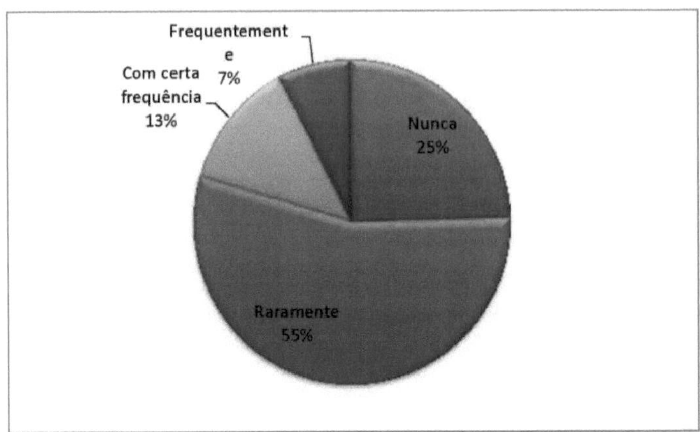

Graph 2 - Observes classroom teaching
Source: Organised by the authors (2017)

Question 3 asked whether the headmaster "uses student performance results to develop the school's educational goals."

Graph 3, on the following page, shows that 28% of respondents said that the headmaster rarely uses student performance to set new educational goals. 12% answered that they do so frequently and a further 9% answered that they do so fairly often. The remaining 21 per cent said never, and another 30 per cent.

Question 4 asked whether the headmaster "makes suggestions to teachers on how they can improve their teaching". The data is compiled in Graph 4, on the following page, and it can be seen that 33 per cent of respondents said that the headmaster suggests changes to improve the teaching that the teacher provides fairly often and 28 per cent of respondents said that he rarely does this.

A further 18 per cent reported that he never makes suggestions and only 10 per cent said that the director does so frequently. The latter was marked exclusively by teachers, totalling 27 of those interviewed. The 11% of respondents who ticked the "Other" option referred only to students, totalling 31% who said they didn't know the answer. No teachers ticked this option.

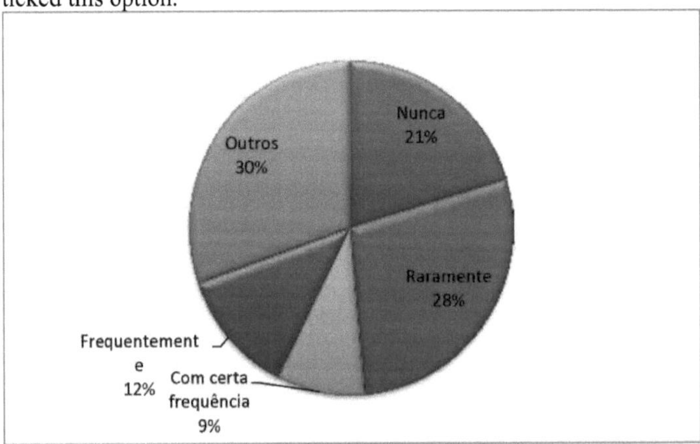

Graph 3 - Develops targets based on previous results
Source: Organised by the authors (2017)

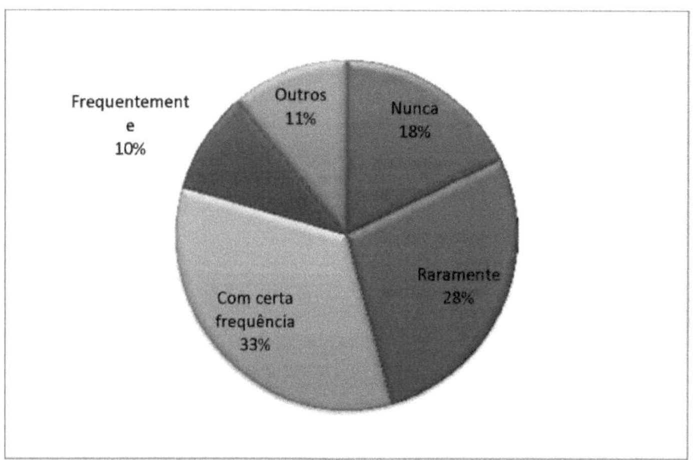

Graph 4 - Gives suggestions to teachers
Source: Organised by the authors (2017)

Question 5 asked whether the Principal monitors the students in their academic and educational work.

Graph 5 on the following page shows that 36 per cent of respondents said that the headmaster monitors the students' work frequently, while 36 per cent said that this happens fairly often.

23 per cent of the teachers and students who took part in the survey said that the Principal rarely monitors students' work and 7 per cent said that he "never" monitors such activity.

It's worth noting here that those who ticked the "Never" box totalled 21 people, and in this percentage of 21 people, only 4 are students and 17 are teachers who say that the management never monitors the students' pedagogical activities.

Two of the teachers wrote: "She doesn't monitor it herself, but she has someone who does it for her" (TEACHER 1), and another wrote: "The headmaster doesn't monitor it, it's the pedagogical coordinator who does it at school" (TEACHER 2). This leads us to understand why the teachers ticked the "never" box.

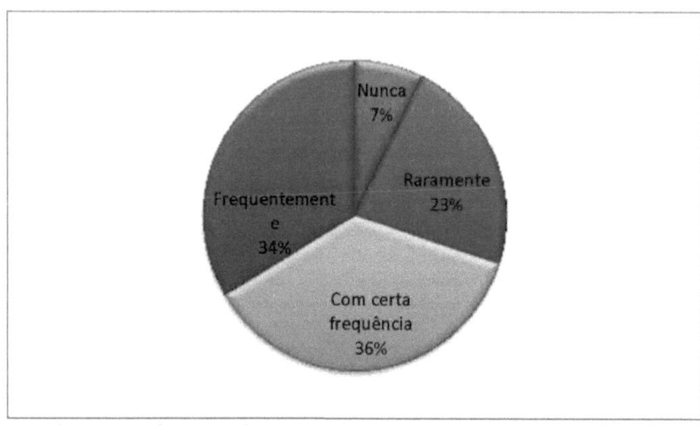

Graph 5 - Monitors students' work
Source: Organised by the authors (2017)

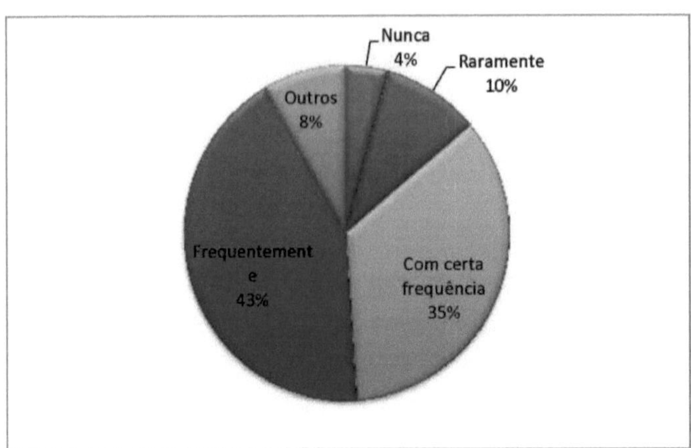

Graph 6 - Discussing problems with teachers

Source: Organised by the authors (2017)

Question 6 asked whether the Principal "When a teacher has problems in the classroom, takes the initiative to discuss the problems.".

Graph 6 shows that the majority of headmasters are in the habit of discussing problems that occur in the classroom frequently (45 per cent) and somewhat frequently (35 per cent).

Only 10 per cent of respondents said that they rarely did and 4 per cent said that they never did. Both, totalling 39 respondents who chose these options, are teachers.

8 per cent of those interviewed, 23 in total (all students), chose to tick the "Other" box, justifying that they couldn't say for sure whether the headteacher discusses problems in the classroom with the teachers.

Question 7 asked whether the headmaster "informs teachers about opportunities to update their knowledge and skills".

Graph 7 shows that 35 per cent of respondents said that the headmaster rarely informs teachers about opportunities to update their curriculum and maintain continuing education. A further 23 per cent replied that this action by the headteacher takes place fairly often.

Only 7% said that he passes on this information frequently and 5% said that he never does so. It should be noted that 21 of the interviewees ticked that option, while 13 chose this one.

As the question was directed at teachers, 30 per cent of those surveyed ticked the "Other" box. This percentage totalled 83 people, including teachers and students.

The majority are students who said they didn't know how to answer the question, others are teachers. One of the teachers who ticked the "Other" box reported:

> We receive all the information about the courses offered by the Municipal Department of Education. The headmaster always informs us of all the events: forums, pedagogical weeks, refresher courses and further training. When there is something outside the municipality, he also directs us to the teacher in the area. (TEACHER 3).

Another explained that: "He passes on information from the Department of Education when he has courses, but apart from that there is no information being publicised at all." (TEACHER 4).

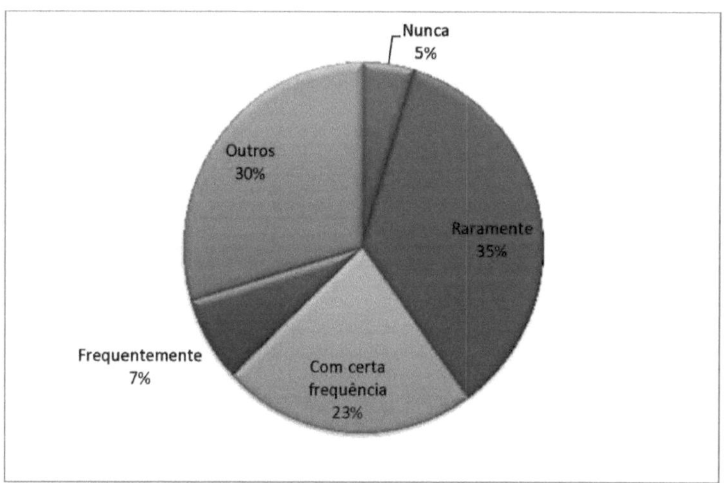

Graph 7 - Informing teachers about new opportunities
Source: Organised by the authors (2017)

Question 8 asked whether the headmaster "pays attention to problems of indiscipline in the classroom." Graph 8 shows that the headmasters of the municipal schools in the city of Caldas Novas, Goiás, are always attentive to indiscipline practised by students. 53% of those interviewed said that managers do this frequently and a further 35% said that they do it fairly often in their schools. 4% said that the headmaster or headmistress is rarely concerned about student indiscipline. Another 8% said that the headteacher never has this kind of concern. It's worth noting here that one of these 8% recorded: "He finds out about what's going on in the classroom, about the mess and the wrong things, because the teacher tells him, not because he keeps an eye on us. Sometimes he keeps an eye on us in the playground." (STUDENT 1). (STUDENT 1). One of the teachers also left a note justifying his choice of "Never". According to him: "This role of 'keeping an eye' on students doesn't fall to the headteacher, but to the coordinator." (TEACHER 5) (TEACHER 5).

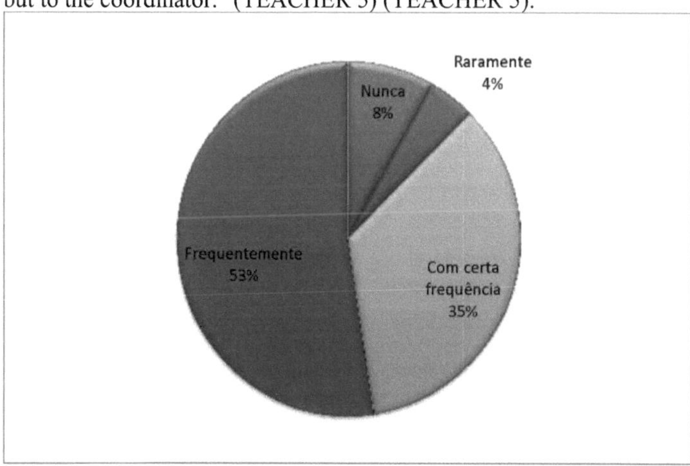

Graph 8 - They pay attention to indiscipline
Source: Organised by the authors (2017)

Question 9 asked whether the headmaster "takes over the classes of teachers who are unexpectedly absent".

Graph 9 shows that 52 per cent said that the head teacher "never" takes over classes in the event of a teacher shortage. A further 24 per cent said that the headteacher does this rarely and 12 per cent reported that he or she does it fairly often.

Only 7% said that managers replace directors frequently and the remaining 5% ticked the "Other" box.

Of particular note here is the statement from two of the interviewees who ticked the "Never" box:

> The headmaster doesn't teach, he just stays in the office. When one of our teachers is absent, the others take the class and we leave early or the coordinator stays with us. (STUDENT 2).

> It's not up to the headmaster to be in the classroom replacing teachers who are absent. That's what the coordinators are there for. Besides, we teachers rotate among ourselves to replace our colleagues" (TEACHER 6).

The highlight here is the student who believes that the headteacher's role is limited to being in his classroom and that this role is insignificant when he says "[...] he only stays in his classroom [...]". There is also the teacher who vehemently states that it is not the headteacher's job to be in the classroom.

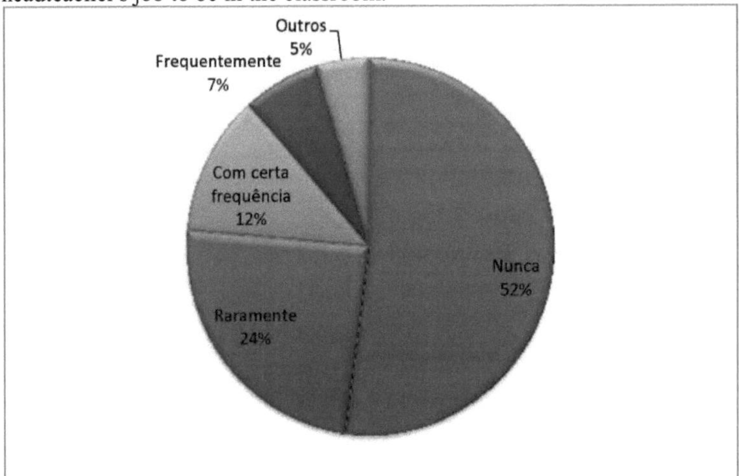

Graph 9 - Taking over classes in the absence of teachers
Source: Organised by the authors (2017)

Graph 10 shows that 44% of those interviewed said that the school manager or headmaster rarely encourages their participation in decisions that he or she is about to make. 23% said that he or she encourages the participation of the school community in decisions that are made fairly often. 19% said that this happens frequently.

However, 10 per cent said that the school's management never encourages this participation. The remaining 4 per cent ticked the "Other" box, mostly students who said they didn't know if the management encouraged it.

Here we would like to highlight the record of one of the teachers:

> The decisions to be made about teaching, practice or anything else related to teaching, yes. But when it comes to financial matters, we teachers are only informed. We don't take part in any decisions to discuss, for example, where the money collected goes. We only find out

A contingent of 27 teachers stated that the school management does not invite them to participate in decisions regarding the school's financial matters.

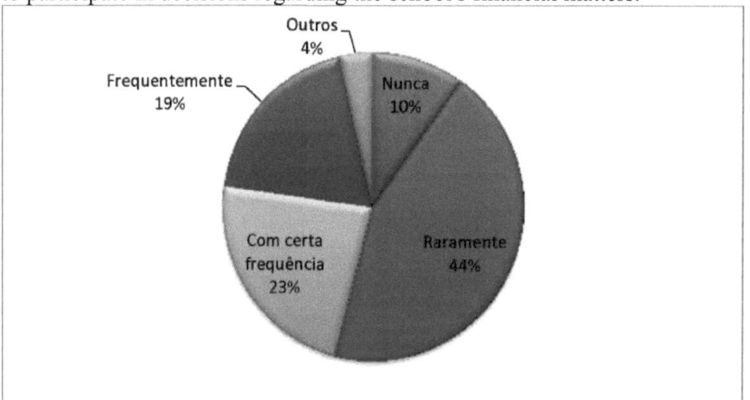

Graph 10 - Encourages the participation of the school community in decisions
Source: Organised by the authors (2017)

Question 11 asked whether the director "is always willing to listen to you.

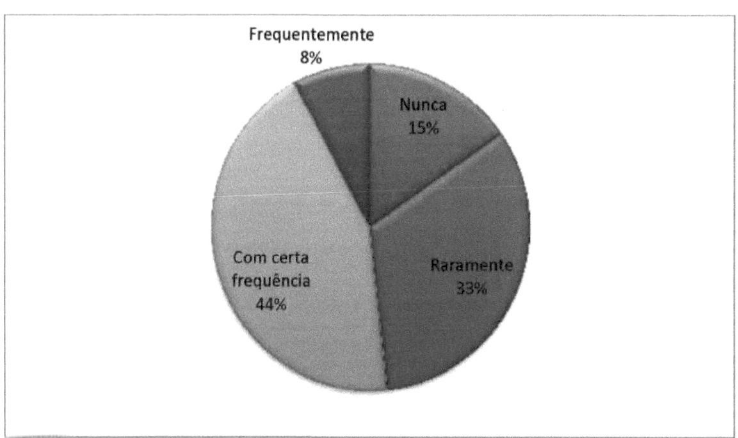

Graph 11 - Attention to students and teachers
Source: Organised by the authors (2017)

Graph 11 shows that 44 per cent said that the headteacher is willing to listen to them on a regular basis. A further 33 per cent said that they listen rarely and 8 per cent said that they listen often.

However, 15 per cent of those interviewed, totalling 43 (including teachers and students), said that the headmaster or headmistress doesn't give them enough attention, explaining that time is the biggest villain.

One of the students said: "The headmaster *is* very good, but when we want to talk to her, she never has time" (STUDENT 3). And one of the teachers said: "He's very attentive, but inside the school it's always a rush, me with my classes and him with his chores, so it's hard to talk" (TEACHER 8).

Question 12 asked whether the headmaster "keeps teachers and students informed about the school's financial resources".

Graph 12 shows that 57 per cent of respondents said that the headmaster never keeps them informed about the school's financial resources. Only 4% replied that they do so frequently.

A further 26% said that managers are rarely informed about the school's financial resources. It is worth emphasising that democratic management, as researched and according to the authors used in the theoretical framework of this study, is one in which the management not only keeps the school community informed, but also makes decisions together with the teachers and students.

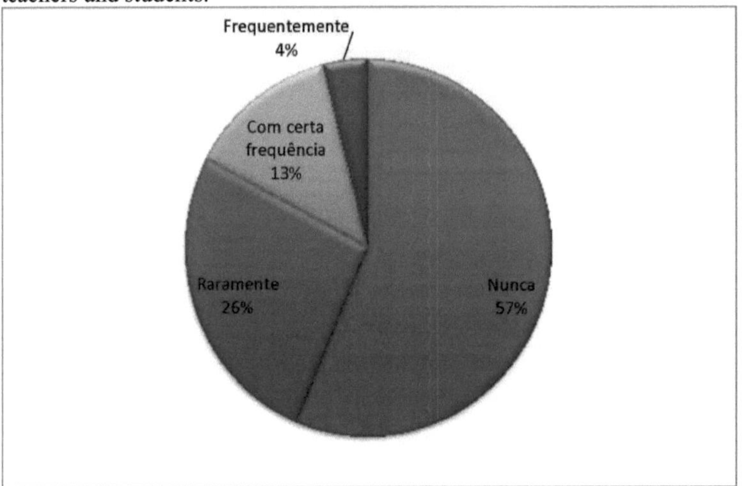

Graph 12 - Information on financial resources
Source: Organised by the authors (2017)

The last question asked what grade the student or teacher would give to the management practised by the current headmaster. The question asked "With 1 being the lowest score and 10 being the highest, what score would you give the management of your school's headmaster?".

Graph 13, on the following page, shows the data relating to this question. Grades (1, 2, 4, 6) were not included because no-one ticked that option. It was decided to separate the grades given by the students from those given by the teachers. This was done with the understanding that evaluating them separately would make it easier to understand how management really works.

Graph 13 shows that there is a discrepancy between the scores given by teachers and students. The lowest score given to management was 3 (three) and only 3 teachers ticked it. The highest mark was 10 (ten) and 121 students chose to mark it, while only 39 teachers gave their headmaster this mark.

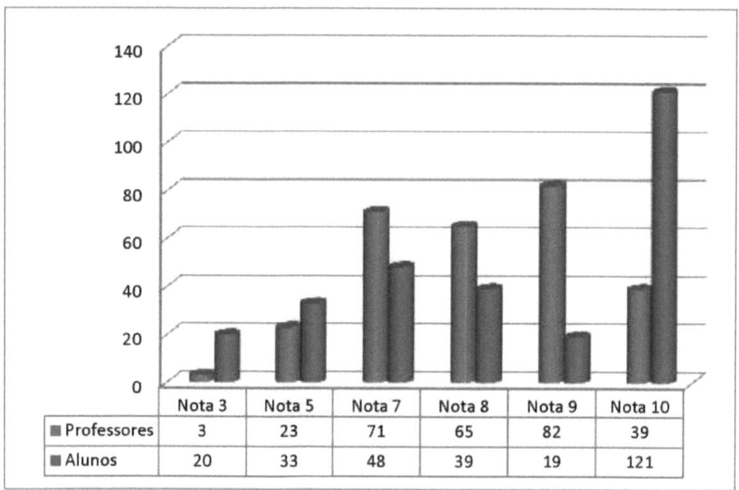

Graph 13 - Student and teacher ratings for management
Source: Organised by the authors (2017)

Graph 13 above also shows that the highest percentage chosen by teachers was grade 9 (nine), while the highest percentage chosen by students was grade 10 (ten).

This discrepancy is due to the fact that the students interviewed are aged between 11 and 15 and have no real concept of what management is. During the survey, we tried to make it clear that the grade was not related to the person of the headteacher, but rather to the administration they have been carrying out.

On the contrary, it is understood that teachers, because they are already adults and know how a school administration or management really works, are more consistent and more reliable in their grades than those offered by students. However, their opinion is not discarded.

4.2 ANALYSIS OF THE INTERVIEW WITH THE DIRECTORS

This chapter will analyse the data collected through the interview with the headmasters of the municipal schools in the city of Caldas Novas-GO. A voice recorder was used with the authorisation of the managers interviewed in order to make the most of it and to check the data collected.

Table 5 was used to compile the data collected during the interview. This data refers to personal information about the headmasters of the municipal schools. The names of the managers have not been used here in order to preserve their image.

Table 5 - Personal details of municipal school managers

N°	SEX	AGE	CIVIL STATUS	CHILDREN
1	F	46	Married	02
2	F	50	Married	02
3	F	41	Married	02
4	F	38	Divorced	01
5	F	57	Married	03
6	F	50	Married	02
7	F	60	Married	03
8	F	41	Married	01
9	F	46	Married	01

10	F	35	Married	03
11	F	47	Married	02
12	F	40	Single	01
13	F	39	Married	02
14	M	49	Married	03

Source: Organised by the authors (2017)

There is only one man in charge of one school, the others are run by women. Their ages range from 35 to 60, with the average being 40. Most of them are married, only one is single and another is divorced. They all have children ranging from 1 to 3, with the majority having at least 2 children.

Table 6 shows the academic qualifications of the headmasters of the municipal schools in Caldas Novas, Goiás.

Table 6 - Directors' academic qualifications

N°	Graduation	Postgraduate	Master's or Doctorate	Specific course for directors
1	Pedagogy	Psychopedagogy	No	Management Education
2	Pedagogy	Teaching Methods and Techniques	No	Educational Administration
3	Pedagogy and Literature	Teaching Methods and Techniques	No	Administrative Management
4	Normal Higher Education (Early Years)	Neuropedagogy	No	Educational Administration
5	Letters	Art History	No	Administration School
6	Pedagogy	Psychopedagogy	No	Administration Education
7	Pedagogy	Psychopedagogy	No	No
8	Pedagogy	Neuropedagogy and Psychoanalysis	No	No
9	Letters	Inclusive education	No	School management
10	Letters	Teaching Higher Education	No	No
11	Pedagogy	Teaching Methods and Techniques and Teaching in Higher Education	No	No
12	Pedagogy	Teaching Methods and Techniques	No	Management Education
13	Pedagogy and Maths	Maths Education and Maths Management	No	No
14	Maths	Teaching Maths	No	No

Source: Organised by the authors (2017)

We can see that all of them are graduates of some kind of degree course, with Pedagogy prevailing, followed by Letters. Only one of them has a degree in Normal Education (formerly teaching) and two of them have a degree in Maths.

All of them are specialised, with the majority specialising in Teaching Methods and Techniques, Teaching in Higher Education and areas related to Psychopedagogy

(Neuropedagogy and Psychoanalysis). The others specialised in specific areas of the degree, such as Mathematics Teaching, Mathematics Management and History of Art.

None of the interviewees have a Master's or Doctorate degree, nor are they even studying for one. There were no reports of them undergoing further training or any other complementary course.

However, item 14.2 of SEMECT's Municipal Education Plan (2013, p. 23-24) states that by 2016 the Secretariat would gradually increase the number of enrolments in postgraduate courses, and to this end it should "[...] implement the offer of postgraduate courses using distance, semi-presential and face-to-face education methodologies, resources and technologies".

I wanted to find out if the headmasters have any specific training in management, given that they were chosen for the job. Table 6 also shows that the majority have degrees in Educational Management, School Administration, Administrative Management, Educational Administration and School Management. However, 6 of them did not have any courses that could help them with school management issues.

The question was whether this current director had been elected or had been appointed to the position. The result of this question can be seen in Graph 14 on the following page.

It can be seen that all the headmasters who manage schools in the city of Caldas Novas were appointed by the "Secretary of Education", none of whom were elected or had taken part in any test or public competition to fill the position.

Graph 14 - Appointment of Directors
Source: Organised by the authors (2017)

The SMECT - Municipal Department of Education, Science and Technology provided the researcher with the document that sets out the "Goals and Strategies" for the 2013 to 2016 management period. The Plan is made up of 20 goals and contains 36 pages. The goals range from pedagogical, political, architectural and socio-economic issues.

In this 2013 Plan, we found the localised item of Goal 19, which states: "ensure conditions, within two (2) years, for the implementation of democratic management of education, associated with technical criteria of merit and performance and public consultation with the school community, within educational institutions." (SEMECT, 2013, p. 32).

It is understood that the proposal was that, since 2015, the choice of headteachers should be made by public consultation with the school community, associated with the candidate's ability and merit. In item 19.1, it is added "respecting national legislation, and jointly considering technical criteria of merit and performance, as well as the participation of the school community, for the appointment of headmasters and headmistresses". (SEMECT, 2013, p. 33).

Items 19.8 and 19.9 of the same document (SEMECT, 2013, p. 34) propose, within two years, or until the end of the term, in 2016: "19.9 Create and develop training policies for the position of headteachers and school managers, consolidating continuing training programmes in the area of management.". It was also established that:

> 19.8) To develop training programmes for permanent teachers in the position of headteachers and school managers, as well as to apply a specific national test, in order to help define objective criteria for filling these positions, the results of which can be used on an ad-hoc basis.

As we already know, this research was carried out between August and November 2016 and so far no specific policy has been found in the municipality for electing or choosing municipal school headmasters.

The Theoretical Framework of this study described the opinion of school management scholars who advocate democratic management, but it is understood that if the headmaster is chosen "solely and exclusively by the Secretary of Education of the municipality" there can be no democracy. The participation of the school community (parents, teachers and pupils) in these choices is advocated, since they are the ones in direct contact with the headteacher and know their capacity and performance better than anyone else.

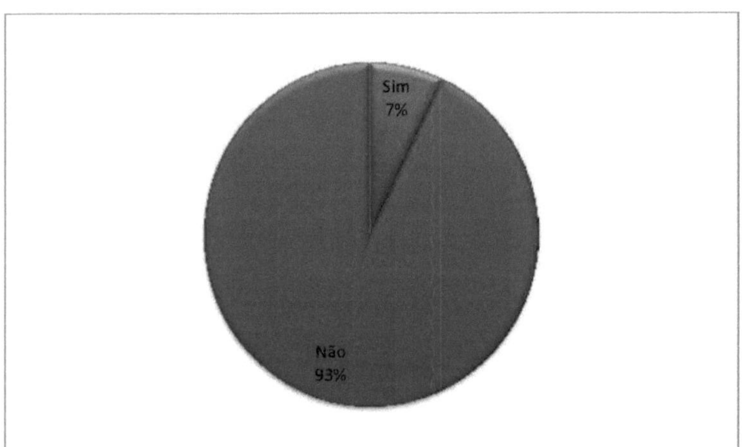

Graph 15 - Student Guild
Source: Organised by the authors (2017)

The headmasters were asked during the interview whether a Student Guild was formed at the school. The result of this question can be seen in Graph 15 above.

This is another target of the SEMECT Plan (2013, p. 33) that has not been met:

> 19.9) Encourage, in all basic education networks, the creation and strengthening of student unions and parents' associations, including ensuring adequate space and operating conditions in schools and encouraging their organic articulation with school councils, through their respective representations.

The School Council is a deliberative and consultative body made up of representatives of parents, teachers, students and staff. Its function is to act, in conjunction with the management team, in the school's pedagogical, administrative and financial management process. We then asked the headmasters if their schools had a School Council, and the results can be seen in Graph 16 on the following page.

During the interview, we tried to find out how the School Council is made up and how it has been working.

In their report, the headmasters clarified that it should be made up of the following proportion: "the following proportion: 40% of teachers; 5% of education specialists, with the exception of the school headmaster; 5% of other staff; 25% of parents; 25% of students." (DIRECTOR 2).

Even though all the schools have a School Council, we can see that it hasn't been carried out as it should be. In all the reports collected from headteachers, it was stated that 50% of parents and pupils don't take part in assemblies very often. According to the interviewees, it is mostly made up of teachers.

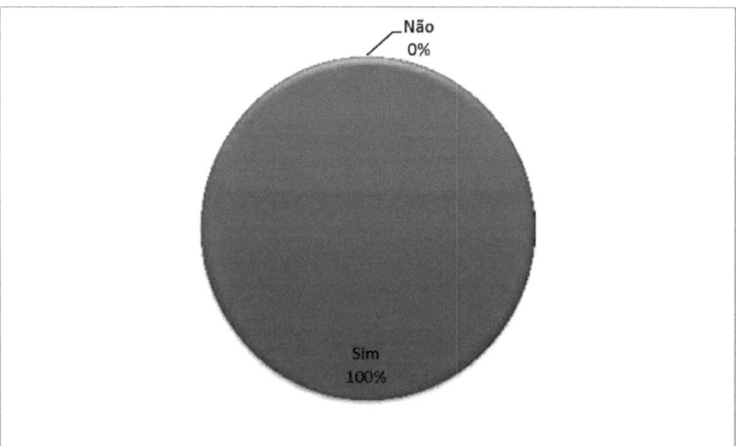

Graph 16 - Presence of a School Council
Source: Organised by the authors (2017)

Strengthening the School Council was also a management goal between 2013 and 2015. SEMECT (2013, p. 33) aims to do the following:

> 19.10) strengthening and encouraging school councils and municipal education councils as instruments of participation and oversight in school and educational management, including through training programmes for council members, ensuring that they are able to function autonomously

The Class Council is a collegiate body that advises and decides on didactic-pedagogical matters. It is based on the Pedagogical Political Project and the School Rules. This team (teachers, pedagogical team and management) meets to discuss, evaluate educational actions and indicate alternatives that seek to guarantee the effectiveness of the students' teaching-learning process.

In view of this, I wanted to find out from the headteacher if there was a Class Council, as can be seen in Graph 17 on the following page.

All the headmasters reported that their school has a class council. They also explained that they meet every two months and in extraordinary assemblies. According to the headteacher, these councils are extremely important for decisions related to student performance. One of the headteachers interviewed said that teachers have to carry out a daily survey of student performance (especially those with learning difficulties) and that they use this report on the day of the council meeting. According to him, "Pedagogical practices are chosen based on this prior diagnosis by the teachers". (DIRECTOR 3).

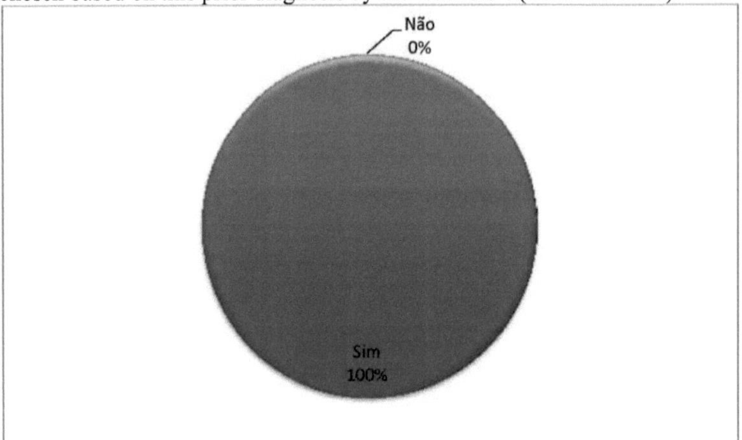

Graph 17 - Presence of a Class Council
Source: Organised by the authors (2017)

I asked the headmasters if they make financial decisions in agreement with the school community. The results are shown in Graph 18 below:

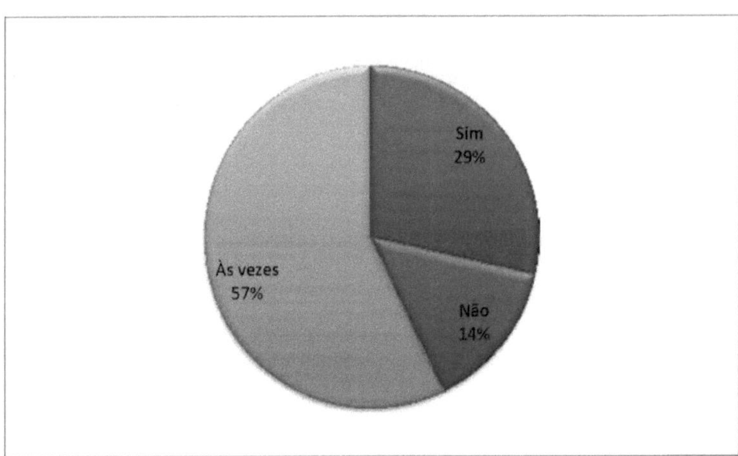

Graph 18 - Democratic management (financial)
Source: Organised by the authors (2017)

Graph 18 shows that the majority of headmasters, totalling 57%, said that they sometimes make financial decisions in agreement with the school community. 29% said that they always make these decisions in agreement with the school community.

together, while 14 per cent assumed that they never make decisions about finances together with parents, teachers and students.

In the targets set by SEMECT (2013, p. 33), the Secretariat aimed to "favour processes of pedagogical, administrative and financial management autonomy in educational

40

establishments" by 2016. This means that the school would be more independent in choosing the allocation of funds, but for this to happen it would be necessary to involve parents, students and teachers, who are the most interested parties.

During the interview, it emerged that the headmasters are former teachers at the school they now manage. Only two (2) of them reported that they were not teachers at that institution. Most of them have been working in education for over 15 years. Only 1 (one) reported that they had only been working for 10 years. Most of the interviewees are in their first appointment as headteachers, with the exception of 3 (two) who have already been headteachers at the same school and another 4 (four) who have already been headteachers at other schools. Both are exclusively dedicated to the job.

Even though all the headmasters interviewed have a good deal of experience and working time, as can be seen in the previous paragraph, when asked if they were aware of SEMECT's Municipal Education Plan (2013-2016) they all said "Yes", but when asked for the plan, for the researcher's verification, none of them had it in their hands and others said "I've read it, but I don't know where to access it, because it's the Municipal Secretariat that uses it, not the schools". It is believed that if a Department of Education establishes a Plan that must be complied with by schools, these institutions should have easy access to it.

The directors interviewed were asked to define the type of management they use. The result is compiled in Graph 19.

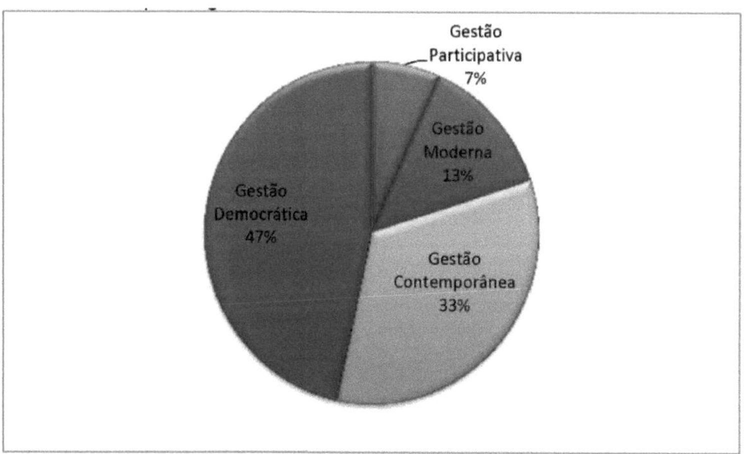

Graph 19 - Directors' type of management
Source: Organised by the authors (2017)

The terms most used in the answers given by the directors were transformed into a graph (GRAPH 19). It can be seen that 47 per cent of those interviewed said that their management was democratic, while a further 33 per cent said that they used the term Contemporary and a further 13% practise Modern management. A small percentage of 7% used the term "Participative" to define their management.

Some of the directors were asked to justify their choice of management. The arguments were all very similar, saying that "I don't do anything alone, every decision is made together". Some people were confused about the terms (Modern, Contemporary and Participative) as if they were synonymous. However, this is not what is stated in the theoretical framework of this study.

The headmasters were also asked whether parents are involved in their management. The results are compiled in Graph 20.

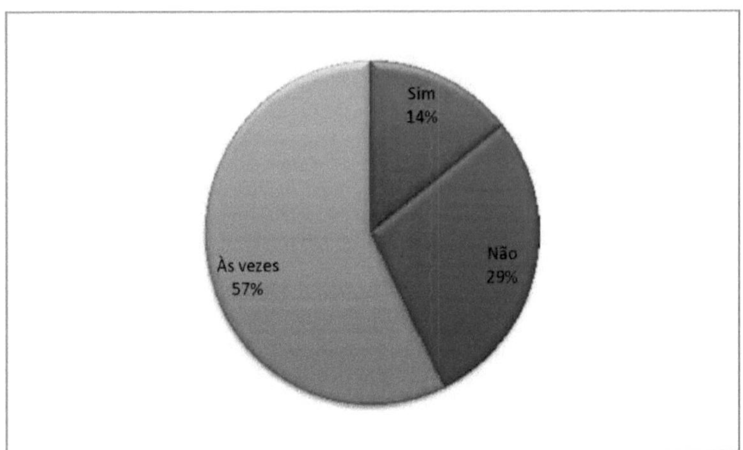

Graph 20 - Participative parents
Source: Organised by the authors (2017)

It can be seen that the majority of headmasters, 57%, said that parents are sometimes involved, while 29% said that parents do not participate in their management. Only 14 per cent said that parents were frequently involved in their school administration.

I wanted to find out from the headmasters what they do to make sure parents are aware of what's going on in the school. Some said that they send "notes", others that they keep a "panel" or "board" with this information at the entrance to the school. But the majority reported using social networks and e-mail to publicise and exchange information with parents.

One of the headmasters said: "Not participating in what happens at school is a culture. For us 'headmasters' to be able to bring parents into the school, we just need to change the way they think."

Most headmasters reported that it is very difficult to get parents to be more present and participative at school. They were therefore asked why this was not the case. They all mentioned the issue of "time". For them, the fact that parents work is the biggest obstacle to more democratic and participatory management.

The headteachers were asked what is most difficult in the day-to-day running of the school. There were a variety of answers, among them: "the lack of support from teachers"; "the lack of help from parents in educating their children"; "the budget, which is too small for the amount of things there is to do"; "the plastering of education, which sometimes prevents us from doing things we want to do"; "the indiscipline and lack of respect students have for us teachers today".

However, it is worth highlighting here a component that was widely reported by the directors: the majority, totalling 10 of the 14 who took part in the survey, reported that "time" is too little for the amount of tasks they have to fulfil on a daily basis.

> I think the rush is the worst thing. I'm the first to arrive and the last to leave every day and I can't cope with the amount of things I have to do. That's because I have constant help from the Pedagogical Coordinator with the students, because if it was just me on my own I wouldn't be able to do it. (DIRECTOR 4).

> It's a lot of work for one person (laughs). The headmaster's job involves much more than sitting in the chair solving problems inside the school. There are lots of meetings outside the school and lots of travelling that we sometimes have to do. At school, then, there are problems with teachers, parents, students, documents that have to be drawn up or executed,

The issue of time is a common complaint from school headmasters. In an interview with Revista Gestão Escolar on 20 October 2016, Luiz Fernando Bronzatto, the headmaster of a school in São Paulo, suggested that headmasters organise their time, use agendas and self-evaluate daily in order to correct the previous day's mistakes.

Another suggestion from Bronzatto is that headteachers or school managers should never be isolated in their offices. For him, the headteacher should accompany the classes taught by the teachers and be present in the schoolyard during breaks. He believes that this interaction makes the manager seen as someone who is accessible to the school community.

To finalise the interview, the headmasters were asked how they believe they are perceived by the teachers and students. Unanimously, they believe that they are well regarded by the school community because they have done a good job.

Some added a detail worth highlighting here. All the headmasters said that it would not be possible to please everyone during their time in office. And some pointed out that when you "call attention to" or "correct" a parent, a student or even a teacher, they generally come to see you as a "bad manager". They also emphasised that this "strong hand" or "firm hand" is necessary for them to be respected and for their work to be successful.

CHAPTER 5

CONCLUSION

This chapter will present the conclusions related to the management of headmasters in municipal schools in the city of Caldas Novas, Goiás. In addition to these conclusions, some recommendations will be made that could help these professionals in their school management process.

5.1 FINAL CONSIDERATIONS

At the beginning of this study, the aim was to find out the profile of the headmasters who manage municipal schools in the city of Caldas Novas, Goiás. The conclusion was that most of them are women, in their 40s, with a degree (mostly in Pedagogy), specialisation in educational areas and good experience (length of service) in education, specifically in the municipality in question.

The question was also asked about the academic background or type of training course and/or exam the headteacher had to take in order to fulfil their role. What was discovered was that the majority of headteachers have a degree in School Management or School Administration, but that a good number of them have a deficit in this training.

The city has a Municipal Education Plan created by the Municipal Department of Education, Science and Technology, instituted in 2013, to be completed by the end of 2016. It was possible to ascertain that headmasters in the city of Caldas Novas-GO do not have direct access to this document. It proposes the appointment of managers based on training and election by the school community, but all those interviewed were appointed to the post by the municipality's Secretary of Education.

Another question that arose at the beginning of this work was how important training in school management was for a school headmaster. During the research, it was possible to realise that headmasters who have this training have an assertive and broad conception of democratic management. They also understand that the participation of parents is of paramount importance to the success of their administration.

The initial hypothesis of this study was that the headmasters in office did not have any training in school management and that this prevented them from carrying out truly democratic management. With regard to training, it was found that 8 of them have this training, while 6 do not. However, it was not possible to relate or prove that this deficit in training is responsible for the lack of democratisation within schools.

The absence of the Children's Guild in municipal schools is proof that the current management has not been democratic. Another item that runs counter to democracy is the low attendance of parents on the School Council and, as reported by the headmasters themselves, their absence from the school itself due to their daily routine and work.

The participation of the school community in the school's financial decisions was also discussed in this paper. Reports from teachers, pupils and the headteachers themselves showed that most decisions in this area are taken by the headteachers in agreement with their management team, without the real or meaningful participation of parents, pupils and even teachers.

It can also be concluded that headmasters are too "stuck" or plastered in their administrative functions and have neglected pedagogical and people management issues. This conclusion was reached due to reports from teachers and students who said that managers had not been following up on teachers' activities; monitoring students; observing classroom teaching; or replacing teachers in their absence.

It is understood that direct and personal contact with teachers, students and parents allows the headmaster to get to know the school and its members better. It is by monitoring classes and constantly circulating in the corridors and courtyards that this manager will be able to identify faults and possible adjustments to be made. What's more, the community will feel more welcome and grateful for receiving the attention they deserve.

It was possible to ascertain that headmasters have not used previous results to develop new targets. These professionals must realise that results management makes school administration more efficient, because it allows them to see what has really worked.

Another item that managers need to pay attention to is their concern for the continuing education of the municipality's teachers. It can't just be limited to the courses offered by the Municipal Secretariat, and this management professional must be aware of new opportunities and inform teachers about them.

The headmasters believe that their management is well regarded by the majority of the school community. This idea was realised when teachers and students were asked to rate the manager. However, there is a point to be discussed. Even though the majority (160 teachers and students) rated their administration with grades 9 and 10, it is worth noting that another 119 teachers and students gave it a median grade of 7 (seven).

It is therefore up to these professionals to get more people involved in their management, making teachers and students more involved in their work.

5.2 RECOMMENDATIONS

The recommendations made in this paper are aimed at the participants in this research. They are therefore recommendations for the teachers, students and headmasters of the municipal schools in the city of Caldas Novas, Goiás.

It is recommended that teachers work democratically in agreement with their school's management. It is understood that this professional is the headmaster's "right-hand man" and that their constant participation in the decisions made by the management will enrich their work and increase the satisfaction rate of the school community. It is recognised that you can't be a teacher in a school and be "against" the management.

As for the students, we recommend that they be more present at school. They should find out how this body works and about the possibilities of setting up a Children's Guild. Through it, students can defend their rights and interests and learn ethics and citizenship in practice. In addition, they will be able to discuss, create and strengthen numerous possibilities for action both in the school environment itself and in the community in which they live.

For headmasters, we recommend that those who don't have a background in school management should seek to supplement their curriculum. Those who already have this background should seek to complement it with courses or Master's and Doctorate degrees. It is understood that continuous learning will make this professional's work more effective.

Managers are also advised to organise their time so that they can carry out their administrative duties and, at the same time, set aside time during the day to monitor classes and pay more attention to parents, teachers and students. It is understood that by doing this, the school community will value their work more.

In addition, headmasters are recommended to encourage parents to take part in the school's daily activities. Encourage students to set up a Children's Guild so that it can be a "support point" for their management. Invite and involve the school community in the decisions you make regarding finances.

REFERENCES

ALVES, L. A. M. History of Education: an introduction. Portugal: University of Porto, 2012.

ARANHA, M. L. A. História da educação. 2 ed. São Paulo: Cortez, 2005.

ARAÚJO, A. C. de. Democratic management of education: the position of teachers. Brasília: University of Brasília, PPGE, 2000.

BASS, B. M. The Bass Handbook of Leadership: Theory, Research & Managerial Applications. 4. ed. New York: Free Press, 2008.

BRAZIL. Constitution of the Federative Republic of Brazil (1988). Available at:

http://www.planalto.gov.br/ccivil_03/constituicao/constituicao.htm. Accessed on 12 June 2016.

. LAW No. 4.024, of 20 December 1961. Available at: http://www2.camara.leg.br/legin/fed/lei/1960-1969/lei-4024-20-dezembro-1961-353722- publicacaooriginal-1-pl.html. Accessed on: 12 June 2016.

. LAW No. 5.692   of 11 August 1971. Available at: http://www2.camara.leg.br/legin/fed/lei/1970-1979/lei-5692-11-agosto-1971-357752- publicacaooriginal-1-pl.html. Accessed on: 13 June 2016.

Law No. 9 .394, of 20   December   1996   ,   available   at
:
http://www.planalto.gov.br/ccivil_03/leis/L9394.htm. Accessed on: 06 June 2016.

Law No.   11   .114, of 16   May   2005   ,   available at   :
http://www.planalto.gov.br/ccivil_03/_ato2004-2006/2005/lei/l11114.htm. Accessed on: 13 July 2016.

______ . How to draw up the School Development Plan - increasing school performance through effective planning. 3. ed. Brasília: FUNDESCOLA/ DIPRO/FNDE/MEC, 2006a.

______ . School education management. Brasilia: Brazil. Ministry of Education. Secretariat for Basic Education, University of Brasilia, Centre for Distance Education, 2006b.

______ . Bill 8.035/2010. National Education Plan for the ten-year period 20112020.   Available at_____ :
<http://www.camara.gov.br/proposicoesWeb/fichadetramitacao?idProposicao=490116>.
Accessed on: 07 July 2016.
DELUIZ, N. Economic globalisation and the challenges for vocational training. Boletim Técnico do SENAC, Rio de Janeiro, v. 22, n. 2, p.15-21, May/August 1996.

DEMO, P. Metodologia do conhecimento científico. São Paulo: Atlas, 2000.

DIAS, E. de P. Concepts of Management and Administration: a critical review. Electronic Journal of Administration. Facef - Vol. 01 - Issue 1 - July-December 2002.

DINO, F. Education, the real bridge to our future. 2017. Available at: http://www.ma10.com.br/minard/2017/01/artigo-educacao-verdadeira-ponte-para-nosso- futuro/. Accessed on: 12 Feb. 2017.

FERREIRA, N. S. C. (Org.). Democratic management of education: current trends, new challenges. Revista Retratos da Escola, Brasília, v. 3, n. 4, p. 273-275, jan./jun. 2009.

FERREIRA, A. B. de H. Dicionário da Língua Portuguesa. 5. ed. Curitiba/SP: Positivo, 2010.

GIL, A. C. Como elaborar projctos de pesquisa. 4. ed. São Paulo: Atlas, 2008.

HONORATO, H. G. The school manager and his competences: leadership under discussion. 2012. Available at   :
<http://www.anpae.org.br/iberoamericano2012/Trabalhos/HerculesGuimaraesHonorato_res_ int_GT8.pdf>.
Accessed on: 12 June 2015.

INEP. National Institute for Educational Studies and Research Anísio Teixeira. Basic Education School Census   2016:   Statistical   Notes.   Available   at: http://download.inep.gov.br/educacao_basica/censo_escolar/apresentacao/2017/apresentac ao_censo_escolar_da_educacao_basica_%202016.pdf. Accessed on: 01 March 2017.

KWASNICKA, E. L. Teoria geral da administração. São Paulo: Atlas, 2003.

LAKATOS, E. M.; MARCONI, M. A. Fundamentos de metodologia científica. 5. ed. São Paulo: Atlas, 2003.

LAWLER III. E. E. Motivation in Work Organisations. In: Bergamini, C.W. (org). Psychodynamics of organisational life. São Paulo: Pioneira, 1990.

LIBÂNEO, J. C. Educação escolar, políticas, estrutura e organização. 2. ed. São Paulo: Cortez, 2005.

______. School Organisation and Management: theory and practice. 5. ed. revised and expanded. Goiânia: MF Livros, 2008.

LOPES, A. P. P. C. School management. Monograph presented to the Pedagogy Course at the Salesiano Auxilium Catholic University Centre, Lins -SP, 2013. Available at: http://www.unisalesiano.edu.br/biblioteca/monografias/56018.pdf. Accessed on: 13 August 2016.

LOPES, N. F. M. A função do diretor do ensino fundamental e médio: uma visão história e atual. Campinas, SP: Dissertation (master's degree) - UNICAMP, Faculty of Education, 2002.
Available at: file:///C:/Users/User/Downloads/LopesN.F.M.pdf. Accessed on: 15 July 2016.

LUCK, H. (Org.) School management and management training. Em Aberto, v. 17, n.72, p. 1195, feb./jun. 2000.

______. Educational management: a paradigmatic question. 3. ed. Petrópolis: Vozes, 2007.

______. Dimensions of school management and its competences. Curitiba: Positivo, 2009.

LUCKESI, C. C. Planejamento e Avaliação na Escola: articulação e necessária determinação ideológica. Série Ideias n. 15. São Paulo: FDE, 1992.

LUPORINI, T. J.; MARTINIAK, V. L.; MAROCHI, Z. M. L. Election and training of municipal school headmasters: legislation and practices in the municipal education network of Ponta Grossa. Revista HISTEDBR on-line, Campinas, SP, n. 43, p. 214-222, Sep. 2011. Available

at: http://www.histedbr.fae.unicamp.br/revista/edicoes/43/art15_43.pdf. Accessed on: 13 September 2016.

MARQUES, M. S. L. L. Taylor and Education in Modern Society. São Paulo: Domínio Público, 2007.

MAXIMIANO, C. A. Teoria geral da administração. São Paulo: Atlas, 2006.

MEC. Ministry of Education. School of Basic Education Managers. Available at: http://portal.mec.gov.br/escola-de-gestores-da-educacao-basica/apresentacao. Accessed on: 13 September 2016.

MEC. Ministry of Education. Secretariat for Basic Education. 2014. Available at: http://portal.mec.gov.br/secretaria-de-educacao-basica/programas-e-acoes. Accessed on: 13 September 2016.

MEC. Ministry of Education. General Coordination of Early Childhood Education. Frequently asked questions about Early Childhood Education. 2013. Available at: http://portal.mec.gov.br/index.php?option=com_docman&view=download&alias=8169- duvidas-mais-frequentes-relacao-educacao-infantil-pdf&category_slug=junho-2011- pdf&Itemid=30192. Accessed on: 13 September 2016.

MEDEIROS, I. Gestão democrática na rede municipal de educação de Porto Alegre de 1989 a 2000: a tensão entre reforma e mudança. Porto Alegre: UFRGS, 2003. Master's dissertation in Education, Federal University of Rio Grande do Sul, 2003.

OLIVEIRA, L. M.; PEREZ JR., J. H.; SILVA, C. A. S. Controladoria estratégica. São Paulo: Atlas, 2002.

PADILHA, P. R. Principals and democratic school management. In: BRASIL, Ministério da Educação e do

Desporto Salto para o futuro: construindo a escola cidadã, projeto político-pedagógico. Brasília: MEC, 1998. p. 67-78.

______. Planejamento Dialógico: Como construir o projeto políticopedagógico da escola. São Paulo: Ed. Cortez, 2001.

PASCOAL, R. What is planning: anticipating activities and situations during the year helps improve teaching and learning and prevents school staff from being taken by surprise by problems. 2014. Available at: https://gestaoescolar.org.br/conteudo/161/o- que-e-planejamento. Accessed on 23 September 2016.

PARO, V. H. Gestão democrática da escola pública. São Paulo: Ática, 2003.

______. Eleição de diretores: a escola pública experimenta a democracia. 2. ed. Campinas: Papirus, 2004.

PENNA, A. G. Introduction to Motivation and Emotion. Rio de Janeiro: Amago, 2001.

PILETTI, C.; PILETTI, N. História Da Educação: de Confúcio a Paulo Freire. 1. ed. São Paulo: Editora Contexto, 2012.

RAMOS, D. K. (Org.). School Council and Democratic Management: Contributions of a Formation for Citizenship. Nova Petrópolis: Nova Harmonia, 2014.

DIGITAL SCHOOL MANAGEMENT MAGAZINE. 5 school management models. 2011. Available at: https://gestaoescolar.org.br/conteudo/504/5-modelos-de-gestao-escolar. Accessed on: 16 September 2016. ROMANELLI, Otaíza de Oliveira. History of education in Brazil. 13. ed. Petrópolis: Vozes, 1991.

SANGENIS, L. F. C. Franciscans in Brazilian education. Petrópolis: Vozes, 2004.

SANTOS, C. R. Educational and School Management for Modernity. São Paulo: Cengage Learning, 2008.

SAVIANI, D. Escola e Democracia. 8. ed. São Paulo: Cortez/Autores Associados, 1985.

SEMEL. Municipal Department of Education and Leisure: contingent of students and teachers. Caldas Novas City Hall. 2016.

SMECT. Municipal Department of Education, Science and Technology: Goals and Strategies. Caldas Novas City Hall (2013 - 2016).

SILVA, V. P. G. da. Wages in the work of Frederick Winslow Taylor. Revista Economia e Sociedade, Campinas, v. 20, n. 2 (42), p. 397-415, Aug. 2011.

BRAZILIAN NATIONAL EDUCATIONAL SYSTEM. OEI - Ministry of Education of Brazil. 2002. Available at: http://www.oei.es/quipu/brasil/estructura.pdf. Accessed on: 20 August 2016.

TAYLOR, F. W. Principles of Scientific Management. São Paulo/SP: Atlas, 1990.

VARGAS, P. A. T. Levels and Modalities of Education and Their Teaching Structures. 2013. Available at: http://www.webartigos.com/artigos/niveis-e-modalidades-da-educacao- e-suas-estruturas-didaticas/111681/. Accessed on: 23 August 2016.

VEIGA, I. P. A. Projeto Político-Pedagógico da escola: uma construção possível. 10. ed. Campinas, SP: Papirus , 2000.

______. Innovations and pedagogical projects: a regulatory or emancipatory relationship? Caderno Cedes, v. 23, n° 61, Campinas, Dec, 2003.

WERLE, F. O. C. Conselhos escolares: implicações na gestão da escola básica. Rio de Janeiro: DP&A, 2003.

I want morebooks!

Buy your books fast and straightforward online - at one of world's fastest growing online book stores! Environmentally sound due to Print-on-Demand technologies.

Buy your books online at
www.morebooks.shop

Kaufen Sie Ihre Bücher schnell und unkompliziert online – auf einer der am schnellsten wachsenden Buchhandelsplattformen weltweit! Dank Print-On-Demand umwelt- und ressourcenschonend produziert.

Bücher schneller online kaufen
www.morebooks.shop

Printed by Books on Demand GmbH, Norderstedt / Germany